Playing For Celtic

Edited
by
Rodger Baillie

STANLEY PAUL
London

STANLEY PAUL & CO LTD
178–202 Great Portland Street, London W.1

AN IMPRINT OF THE  HUTCHINSON GROUP

London Melbourne Sydney
Auckland Bombay Toronto
Johannesburg New York

First Published 1969

*This book has been set in Imprint type face. It has been
printed in Great Britain at Taylor Garnett Evans &
Co. Ltd by offset Lithography in Watford, Hertfordshire*

09 098760 8

Contents

Introduction

The three most important trophies in Scottish football – the League championship award, the Scottish Cup and the League Cup – sit, highlights gleaming, on a solid, homely, display cabinet in the boardroom at Celtic Park.

They are surrounded by an impressive display – and I am sure a cleaners' headache – of the permanent collection of presents collected on foreign trips, and of the reminders of past glories, the Empire Exhibition trophy, the Coronation Cup, and the most famous of all, the replica of the European Cup.

For the second time in three seasons Celtic have achieved a clean sweep of all the Scottish honours and these three giant pieces of silver are the testimony to the most important part of any football club, their present team.

All famous football clubs proudly talk about tradition, some more than others.

It is almost indefinable, a quality interwoven with old men's memories of great names and great games to its continuing starting point, kids kicking a ball in the street saying they want to play for one team.

It is a simple, but too obviously overlooked fact, in the jungle of present-day soccer, that not every team can win an honour.

Yet it is dangerous for a top side to go too long without winning any award, the glories of the past or the promise of the future do not compensate fans for ever.

Celtic supporters have known their years of supporting a side whose potential always outmatched their performance . . . they call them the 'lean years' now at Parkhead.

That is why these three trophies are so important to the club. They represent something that can be looked at, something that can be touched, a reward for a slog through nearly fifty matches in the home tournaments to the undisputed title of Scotland's number one team.

They have won twelve major trophies at Parkhead since Jock Stein returned to revolutionise Celtic, and Scottish football.

It includes Europe's number one trophy, the European Cup, the league championship, four times, the Scottish Cup three times, and the League Cup four times.

That amazing list may cause even our future footballers – hurrying to play soccer in space just as today we jet over Europe – to stop and wonder.

If you take last season alone which of the three Cups in that board-room is the most important to Celtic? . . . It would be very hard to separate them.

The League Cup has rested solidly on the same spot at Parkhead for four seasons, taken away only for the short journey to Hampden and back.

A wonderful tribute to the starting power of Celtic to capture the trophy which is the first to be competed for every season.

The Scottish Cup sits in the middle. The green-and-white ribbons still tied on it from the April afternoon when it was presented to Billy McNeill at Hampden.

It is there for a record-breaking twentieth time, all the more sweeter for Celtic fans because it was won in one of the peaks of the season, the 4–0 victory against Rangers in the final.

But perhaps the trophy which gives everyone at Parkhead the most satisfaction is the League championship.

Apart from a spell before and during the First World War—and really the only significance these records have in relation to modern football is that they are a target to be knocked down – the image of Celtic was of a side more associated with Cup competitions.

It was said, and sometimes not too kindly, that they could raise their game for five or six matches a season, but not for the long league campaign.

Someone once said that Scotland is the only country where you can get the four seasons in one day, and certainly our footballers have to be attuned to more weather changes than in almost any other country.

The league is the long grind from August to April, the fixtures that have to be played in all weathers and despite the pressure of all other matches, whether it is European or domestic Cup competitions.

To win it four times in a row in the pressure-cooker of modern soccer is something which may itself be a record for a long time.

At the end of the season I asked Celtic manager Jock Stein what had pleased him most about the team in his spell at Parkhead and he answered in one word . . . 'consistency'.

Then he elaborated: 'I am pleased that we have changed the club's image to add that quality to our league matches which we always had in Cup competitions. Nobody can say now we are a team who only touch the top in a few matches a season.'

The statistics to support that statement are slightly staggering. Only ten defeats in 136 league games over the last four seasons.

No wonder a proud Celtic chairman, Sir Bob Kelly – in the season he was knighted by the Queen – could describe it later as: 'The outstanding performance of modern football.'

And for a man whose time in football spans more than half a century he paid a glowing tribute when he said: 'I'm even happier that the trophies have been won in an exciting and entertaining fashion.

'But the consistent success in the league championship must be the outstanding achievement. I certainly feel that it equals anything in the past history of the club.

'That consistency which eluded us for so long arrived at Parkhead with our manager, Mr. Stein, who has been an inspiration in his leadership.

'Despite the fact that this team have two to go to equal the number of league championships of that record-breaking team early in the century, I feel their performance is at least equal in merit to those former achievements.

'The demands both physically and mentally are that much higher in present-day football.

'Today it is not just a question of playing in league matches and possibly three at the most international matches. The team of today has to win the title and also play many extra matches.'

What was special about the fourth championship win? I would label it the season of the great come-back, especially after the crushing the players' morale took after the European Cup defeat by A.C. Milan, the biggest disappointment of the season.

Perhaps throughout the season Celtic never hit the long stretches of superbly exciting soccer which marked their play in some other

8

seasons, and the graph of their form – but not their points total – tended to rise and dip.

But what a triumph it was for their spirit, for an ability never to accept defeat!

In key games, such as Hibs at Easter Road – the best league game I saw all season – Dundee United at Tannadice, St. Johnstone at Muirton, Airdrie at Parkhead and Kilmarnock at Rugby Park, they either came from behind to draw or snatch a win in the most crucial time of the last ten minutes.

The reserve side got into the act as well. They won the Reserve League Cup and assistant manager Sean Fallon wrote in the club newspaper that it was pleasing that they had done well in the reserve competition with some of their younger players – the lifeblood for the future – showing a lot of promise.

What of the future? Stein, never given to extravagant predictions, says cautiously: 'We are better prepared than ever.'

And he points to Harry Hood as one of the forwards he expects will become a key-man next season and he looks for an improvement from the other new signing, Tom Callaghan, who had an unhappy first season after his move from Dunfermline, now that he lives in Glasgow.

Sir Bob Kelly, who has known every variation in the fortunes of his club, said sensibly: 'A club can never really reach the top, there is always a higher pinnacle.

'But it would be stupid to imagine that we can go on winning the championship and all the top honours indefinitely every season.'

But the fact that the majority of the first team pool are still in their middle twenties is a sign that while Celtic fans may not have the chance to cheer the winning of three trophies every season the honours parade at Parkhead could be going on for a long time yet.

Jim Craig

I'm the odd man out at Celtic! For my life in football is different from the rest of the first-team pool . . . I am a part-time full-timer.

Let me explain just what that means. I combine my job as a footballer with a career as a dentist.

The old idea of a part-time player who trained twice a week in sessions which he managed to squeeze in after his work has no place in modern football.

I train with the rest of the first-team every morning, I am available for any extra sessions and any foreign competitive matches which we play.

However if the team are going perhaps for a golf outing, or a few days relaxation at their coast headquarters, then I am excused attending it.

I am lucky in that, as a dentist, I am able to combine two roles in my life. But I would like to stress that as far as football is concerned I am a full-timer in attitude and approach.

This is my second spell at Celtic Park . . . I must say it has produced more medals than the first time.

I went to Celtic straight from school, and as an amateur played in their third team. Then, when I was in my second year as a dental student, I found it impossible to carry on with my football.

I played only for Glasgow University for a spell after that – I even had a few games in goal – and I was picked for the Scottish Universities against England.

I had played mostly at right-half for the University, and it was in

Head down, face screwed up in concentration, another game for Jim Craig as he takes the field to try to help Celtic towards victory.

January 1965 that I received another invitation to join Celtic, and returned . . . as a right-back.

This is an exciting time to be in football. I believe it is changing in many ways, and one of them is in my own position, full-back.

People say football is a simple game . . . I don't think it is!

Maybe it was in the old days when it was just a question of a defence against an attack. Now there are so many systems that you need intelligent planning to combat them.

It may look simple to the fans, and if it is successful it certainly should appear that way. But I don't think many fans realise how much work goes on behind the scenes nowadays.

The old ideas of numbers on a jersey which meant a forward played upfield, and a defender at the back have gone for ever.

Unfortunately too many fans cannot get rid of this idea. When I am a spectator I sometimes feel sorry for a player whom the crowd feels is not fulfilling his position the way they want.

They forget that he may be playing the role exactly the way his manager has laid down, and within the team plan.

I know my own style is not popular with some of the Celtic fans. They want to see a full-back who dives into the tackle.

I prefer to wait if possible so that the chance is not 50–50, but 70–30 in my favour to get the ball, especially if I managed to force the winger to the bye-line.

Let me give you an example of how we can be asked to play to instructions, and the onlooker does not see everything.

I was criticised by one Sunday paper journalist after the European Cup tie against A.C. Milan in Glasgow as 'having probably the least effective game of my career'.

I had been detailed to mark their danger man, Piero Prati, and he had only once got away from me, when he moved inside as I took a throw-in.

The journalist wrote that I showed how not to play Prati . . . I wonder what he thought about the Ajax full-back in the European Cup Final when the Italian winger scored a hat-trick.

European football has always interested me. Maybe it is because I played in four European Cup Winners Cup ties before I even took part in a Scottish Cup tie.

The great difference between that Celtic side – it was in 1966 when we reached the semi-final of the Cup Winners and were then beaten by Liverpool – and the side of today is in attitude.

We have almost the same pool of players, but then there were some teams we feared, maybe even secretly hoped we could dodge in any draw.

12

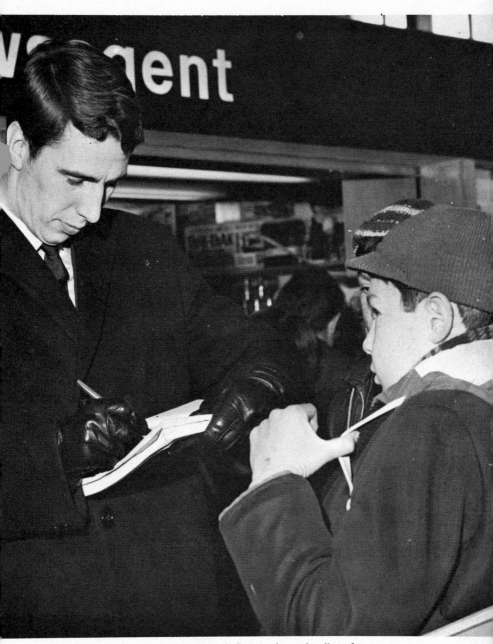

Signing on time . . . another autograph for another schoolboy from right-back Jim Craig, the routine as familiar to soccer's stars as playing the game itself.

Now we are on equal terms, at least, with any of them. Why not? If it had not been for that one unfortunate breakaway we might have been European champions again.

I must admit it hit me when I was watching the match between A.C. Milan and Ajax on television. The Scottish Cup Final victory against Rangers was a great moment for our fans . . . I know they probably rate that the high spot of the season.

But I think the time has come when we must look beyond Scotland, and really European success in the long run is the greater award.

There are other differences in Europe. Celtic were one of the great pioneers of attacking full-backs . . . remember Tommy Gemmell's equaliser in Lisbon.

Now, other teams try to counteract it. I noticed last season that every time I moved up to support the attack – and remember I am the defending full-back – I was shadowed by the winger.

It happened with Dzajic of Red Star Belgrade and also Bereta, the left-winger of French champions St. Etienne. He missed me only once, when I managed to break away and score at Parkhead . . . one of the three goals I scored last season.

And with that grand total I topped my own personal scoring average.

It was nice to turn goal-taker instead of goal-maker, although that role has had its memorable moments, especially in the European Cup Final against Inter-Milan in Lisbon, when I gave my full-back partner Tommy Gemmell the pass from which he scored his wonderful equaliser.

We had been given the role of pulling the ball back into the path of the half-backs or forwards if we went upfield, to try to get it past the wall of the Inter defence.

A few minutes before Tommy scored there was another move when I passed to Bobby Murdoch, but he was not quite expecting the ball, it went to his left foot and the shot went past.

Yet if it had not been for a decision of manager Jock Stein's in an earlier tie I would not have been in Lisbon.

During the middle of that season I had not been playing well, things had started to go badly for me after Christmas.

When we went to Yugoslavia to take on Vojvodina in the quarter-final I really expected to be dropped. It was such a vital time – we were still involved in three competitions – that I realised that if I lost my place then it would probably be for the rest of the season.

However I was fortunate for although we lost 1–0 I had been picked

Mr. and Mrs. . . . Jim Craig, the last batchelor in the Celtic first team with his bride, Elizabeth Farrell, after their wedding in June.

for the match, and had played reasonably well enough to keep my place.

Two full-backs combining for that goal in Lisbon – with the help of a pass from a wing-half, Bobby Murdoch to start it off – would have been a soccer rarity ten years ago.

But now football is in such a state of change that every position has to contribute something different . . . in an effort to break down defensive systems.

Eventually I predict all this planning and counter-planning will result in a new style of football, where positions will mean even less than they do now.

I have noticed on TV that if Eddie McCreadie dashes upfield with Chelsea, he does not have to chase back, someone slots in behind him.

Every team uses a cover method to some extent. But eventually I see no reason why a full-back should not stay upfield for as long as five minutes if someone else is in his position.

There won't be a basic system then, players will be specialists who can fit in to almost any position.

Changes are already on the way. The British and Continental styles are beginning to merge.

We are borrowing from them, and they are copying us. The Continentals are tackling more . . . did you watch the way A.C. Milan tackled in the European Cup Final against Ajax, it was just as hard as any British side.

And now in Britain there is more shielding of the ball to stop your opponents getting to it. That is keeping your back to an opponent, so as he cannot tackle.

I am convinced this is the reason for the higher rate of fouls especially in England.

Perhaps some time really hard tackling will be eliminated from the game. It will never disappear – it is too much part of football's framework – but I see the emphasis going more on interception.

Even though I am the defensive full-back of the Celtic team, I prefer to intercept if it is at all possible.

Every full-back has various styles of wingers whom he does not like to play against . . . I must admit I would hate to have to play such a close-dribbling stylist as Jimmy Johnstone.

Hibs left-winger Eric Stevenson is one of the club wingers in Scotland whom I respect very much, and in Europe I can only say I'm glad I was against Gento, of Real Madrid, when he was supposed to be past his best.

He and I were opponents when Celtic played Real Madrid in the benefit match for Alfred Di Stefano. Gento might have been on the way down then but he was still extremely fast.

I look forward to these European matches most of all. I am a player who needs to be mentally under pressure . . . and with the rest of the Celtic team I have come to look forward to the European matches. I like these big games.

Football in Scotland will always be vital to us . . . but it is in Europe that the significant tactical developments will take place.

And it is in Europe that a team's real stature is measured. Any side could win domestic trophies in their own country for season after season and still be relatively unrecognised, but one victory in the European Cup Final makes them known all over the world.

Look how Lisbon established Celtic on the soccer map! Every member of the Parkhead staff wants to repeat that victory . . . and you can bet that we will have a few tactical surprises ourselves to help us to that goal.

The League

The winning margin in Celtic's successful League Championship campaign last season was the biggest of their four flag victories . . . a five-point lead over their nearest rivals, Rangers.

So on the statistical evidence it appears to have been an easier win than in any of the other three seasons.

But after the title had been signed, sealed and delivered to Parkhead manager Jock Stein looked back over the thirty-four match programme and said:

'I don't think it was any easier. It was a better league all round, and a harder one. No team went through undefeated – or even looked like it – and that's a healthy sign.'

It seems more and more that it will be the 'Old Firm' clubs, with their vast financial resources, who will monopolise the honours in Scotland.

And with such a monopoly the charge is often made from England that it is too easy for Celtic and Rangers and that a weak league produces weak champions.

This was killed when Celtic beat every other British club to win the European Cup, but it is raised again after bad performances, such as this season in the international championship, by the Scottish team.

But Stein is a vigorous champion of Scottish football and he told me: 'Our standards are not half as bad as they are made out. Airdrie took five points off the 'Old Firm' and Kilmarnock took four.

'That does not seem to show a complete monopoly in every fixture. The difference is often not in ability, but in atmosphere.

It's all over . . . and the Kilmarnock players applaud Celtic stars,
including Billy McNeill and Tommy Gemmel, as they walk off Rugby Park
after the 2–2 draw, and the point which clinched yet another
league championship.

'I know what it's like to be manager of a provincial club and play in front of small crowds. That's why all teams lift their game when they play Celtic or Rangers, but often too they cannot keep it up.

'You rarely ever go to an English First Division match without seeing big crowds. Our game suffers from the lack of them.'

What is the solution to the problem? Celtic chairman Sir Bob Kelly has put forward the suggestion of amalgamations with one club representing each county.

But the mills of soccer grind slowly, and no one could forecast when such a radical step would ever be carried through.

However, the present dominance by the 'Old Firm' means that while they may not have the same intense pressure as the English League sides it is balanced by the fact that they are often competing on two or three fronts at one time.

Frequently a team is involved in the later stages of a European competition, and fighting also to capture the domestic trophies.

For Celtic the worst moment in the entire season came with the European Cup defeat from A.C. Milan.

They had led the league from the middle of October and it seemed just before Christmas it would be a runaway victory.

But league championships are not wrapped up by December. Celtic, on frozen grounds, dropped three points in succession to Falkirk, Kilmarnock and Airdrie, and then another two to Rangers at Ibrox.

However, they valiantly stuck to a narrow lead from 4 January until 24 March. The one time it looked in real danger was after that Milan defeat.

They were due to play Partick Thistle at Parkhead. Stein described it later as the 'club's worst league match in four seasons' but they still won 1–0, and kept that points lead at the top of the table.

Then on 24 March came the first break in the deadlock between the big two in the championship chase.

Both had fixtures which looked likely to give them full points. Celtic against Hibs at Parkhead, Rangers away to Airdrie at Broomfield.

Both failed to take their two points, but the Rangers slip was the greater. They dropped two points in a 3–2 defeat from Airdrie while Celtic were drawing 1–1 with Hibs.

And when in their next mid-week fixture Celtic snapped back against St. Johnstone from being down 2–0 at half-time to win 3–2 with a last-minute goal, it was virtually over.

Stein looked back to say it was the one which possibly clinched the

The goal that won a title . . . and the man looking intently as his
last-minute equaliser flashes into the net against Kilmarnock at
Rugby Park is left-back, Tommy Gemmell.

league for Celtic, it showed the opposition that they were not prepared
to surrender the championship without a fight.

So let us examine month-by-month the championship trail which
started at Shawfield in September and ended thirty-four league games
later at Dens Park, and both of them away victories.

And collectors of odd soccer facts might care to note that not once
in the four championship victories have Celtic clinched it on their own
Parkhead.

The first season it was wrapped up at Motherwell, the second time
against Rangers at Ibrox, two seasons ago against Dunfermline at
East End Park and last year at Rugby Park against Kilmarnock.

There were four league matches in September, and it was not the
most memorable month as they started their defence of the title, for in
only one match – the first against Clyde at Shawfield – was there a
decisive result.

That was a 3–0 victory with goals from Brogan, Lennox and
Gemmell. The next match was a 4–2 defeat from Rangers at Parkhead.

It was a match where Rangers took a two-goal lead then Wallace
pulled one back and Celtic bitterly contested an offside decision

against a goal by Lennox which would have given them the equaliser.

Penman made it 3–1 in the second-half, then Wallace brought the score back to 3–2 before Willie Johnston scored a fourth in the last minutes.

Celtic squeezed in a European Cup-tie against St. Etienne and then went to one of their toughest away assignments, Dunfermline at East End Park.

The Fifers scored first through right-half Jim Fraser and then Jimmy Johnstone equalised in the second-half.

The month ended with a 2–1 home victory against Aberdeen, and a controversial goal 15 minutes from time by Bobby Lennox, although Dons' 'keeper Bobby Clark claimed he had been fouled. The first goal came from George Connelly.

It was still fairly mixed in October, although only one point was dropped, to Morton at Greenock.

Celtic started with a sound 2–0 win and goals from Murdoch and Gemmell, against Dundee United – then league leaders – at Parkhead. This was the match in which Jimmy Johnstone was substituted, and later suspended by the club for a week.

The next week they were at Tynecastle, and without Johnstone and John Hughes, a 'flu victim, they won through with a Steve Chalmers header against Hearts.

The first of the three clashes with St. Johnstone followed, a 2–1 victory at Parkhead with the goals coming from Lennox and McNeill.

The one point they dropped this month was at Greenock, when Joe McBride scored but Joe Harper equalised . . . still they now had a one-point lead at the top of the table against St. Mirren.

November was one of the key months for Celtic. They swept off their somewhat uncertain form, and as rivals Rangers dropped points, they collected a full ten out of five games.

It started with a 3–1 victory against Dundee at Parkhead, the goal-scorers were Johnstone, and Steve Chalmers, two.

Then they went to Arbroath and rattled in five goals against the bottom-of-the-league side. The scorers were Chalmers, with a hat-trick, and McNeill and Wallace.

Bobby Murdoch got the two goals in the victory against Raith Rovers at Parkhead, and the Kirkcaldy club's 'keeper, Bobby Reid, was sent off by referee John Gordon.

Then there was a crushing 4–0 win against Partick Thistle at Firhill, and a scoring debut for new signing Tom Callaghan when he grabbed the second goal. The other scorers were John Hughes, twice, and Lennox.

Two defenders crowd round him, the 'keeper makes a despairing dive . . .
but none of them can stop John Hughes powering the ball into the back
of the net for Celtic's fourth goal in a 5–0 win against St. Mirren.

And on the last day of the month came one of the most memorable
matches of the season, a 5–2 victory against Hibs at Easter Road.

Celtic had taken the lead with a Gemmell penalty, but then Joe
McBride had equalised against his old club, and in 75 minutes the
champions were struggling when Joe Davis scored for Hibs with a
penalty.

And then this amazing Celtic side struck to transform the score-
line, with four goals inside ten minutes.

Billy McNeill started it, Hughes got the next, then Lennox and finally Hughes the fifth . . . irresistible soccer.

And they whirled into December with a 5–0 victory against St. Mirren, all the goals – from Chalmers, two, Johnstone, Hughes and Gemmell, penalty – were scored in the second-half as the crowd chanted 'champions'.

But they were a little premature. The first bad weather of the season came as they slithered to a goal-less draw against Falkirk at Brockville, the first point they had dropped in eight weeks.

Then they could only draw 1–1 with Kilmarnock at Parkhead, despite a barrage at the Ayrshire side's goal . . . Chalmers got the goal.

And it was stalemate again the next week with a 0–0 draw against Airdrie at Broomfield.

However, January started with a knighthood for Sir Robert Kelly, and a 5–0 victory against Clyde at Parkhead to celebrate it. The scorers were Callaghan, two, Gemmell, penalty, Wallace and Lennox.

The next day came the second league defeat by Rangers, this time at Ibrox. It took a controversial penalty decision by referee Archie Webster in 75 minutes and from which John Greig scored, to give the Ibrox side victory, but Rangers were the more impressive side.

Celtic picked up again when Dunfermline went to Parkhead on 4 January, and Wallace scored two goals and Lennox one in a 3–1 win.

They demolished Aberdeen at Pittodrie, always one of the toughest away fixtures. The scorers were Hughes, Wallace and Boel, own goal.

And followed up with another magnificent away victory, two of the toughest assignments any team could be given, when they won 3–1 at Tannadice.

It was a marvellous performance by John Hughes, who gave Celtic a 2–1 lead in 85 minutes after Dundee United had equalised a Bobby Lennox goal, and Pat McMahon got the third.

The pitch was a patchwork of clinging mud, the rain lashed down, but both teams turned it into a wonderful match.

An Italian TV team was at Parkhead for the next league game on 2 February – when after a break for the Scottish Cup – Celtic slammed Hearts 5–0 with goals from Lennox, Wallace, Murdoch, Johnstone and Brogan.

There was a winter weather break after that, and with Scottish Cup matches it was not until 5 March that they were back on league business with a 7–1 crushing of Arbroath and their biggest league win. There was a hat-trick for Wallace, two for Chalmers and Johnstone, and Hughes completed the scoring.

Celtic then had a hard away fixture at Kirkcaldy, when they played with their mind obviously on the Milan match the following week. They won 3–1, although Raith scored first and the scorers were Wallace, two, and Auld.

After the midweek Milan match, John Hughes helped Celtic scramble to a 1–0 victory against Partick Thistle at Parkhead.

Hibs finally took the first point off Celtic since the Ibrox defeat with a shock 1–1 draw and Joe McBride scored his second goal against his old club. Wallace got Celtic's goal.

They overwhelmed St. Mirren with a 3–0 victory and goals from Craig, Hughes and new boy Harry Hood in his first game.

Then came the epic victory at St. Johnstone, a 3–2 win at Muirton with goals from Wallace, Gemmell, and Hood.

Now they were on the home straight to the championship, and beat relegation-bound Falkirk 5–2 at Parkhead, when Lennox with two goals, one from a penalty, Wallace, two, and Hood scored.

They should have wrapped it up against Airdrie at Parkhead. But at one time the Broomfield side led 2–1, and there were bitter protests when a last-minute goal by Billy McNeill was disallowed. Gemmell, penalty, and Lennox got the goals which did count.

And then against Kilmarnock at Rugby Park they finally finished the race, although there was an outside chance that if they lost their two remaining games, and Rangers won theirs by a large total, they could have been pipped on goal average.

It was a shaky start for Celtic, they were down 2–0 at half-time. Then Killie skipper Frank Beattie headed at Bobby Murdoch lob into his own net, and Gemmell scored the league winner right on time to make the score 2–2, and give them the point they needed.

The Parkhead match against Morton was the season's biggest anti-climax. The team paraded in front of their three trophies at the start, then were defeated 4–2. The scorers were Wallace and Hood.

But they finished with a victory against Dundee at Dens Park when Macari and Hood scored in a 2–1 victory.

The Jimmy Johnstone Show

For the football fans and players who believe in omens – and which of us doesn't even if it's only slightly? – the rearranged European Cup draw was a good sign.

It put Celtic against the current kings of French football, St. Etienne, instead of Ferencvaros, the Hungarian team they had been supposed to play.

The successful European Cup campaign of 1967 had included a victory against the then reigning French champions, Nantes . . . was soccer history going to repeat itself?

But the signs were soon to go wrong!

Yet again the new campaign started with an outward show of normality, those inevitable spy trips that are now so much of the soccer scene before the actual games.

Jock Stein hurried off to France to watch St. Etienne play and sent his assistant manager, Sean Fallon to Dublin to watch the Scottish League – with six Celtic players – take on the League of Ireland at Dalymount Park.

And it was in Dublin in one of those almost meaningless fixtures which still clutter the calendar, that the first disaster struck.

Bobby Murdoch, possibly the most indispensable member of the Celtic first-team pool, was injured in the 0–0 draw in Dublin.

Carefully he was carried off between the trainer Tom McNiven and Tom Callaghan, soon to be his team-mate, just before half-time with damaged ligaments.

There were still two weeks to go to the first game against St.

Their positions were the same but their eras were different. Two of the most famous men ever to wear the number seven strip of Celtic chat about the outside-right position as Jimmy Delaney (*left*) pours a cup of tea for Jimmy Johnstone.

Etienne in France, and the race was on to get Murdoch fit . . . but it was a race he was to lose.

St. Etienne then sent off their spy to Parkhead, a tall, pipe-smoking, Maigret-style Frenchman, Pierre Garonnaire, right-hand man of coach Albert Batteaux.

In those dim days a decade ago when the European Cup, and the other Continental competitions, were only soccer infants still struggling for a permanent place on the football calendar, the spy trips were kept secret.

But now they are more likely to be made with a flock of reporters accompanying the spy, and an official of the opposition team waiting at the airport.

Garonnaire saw two Celtic matches, and if he had stayed all season it's doubtful if he would have watched a greater contrast.

The first was a goal-scoring romp, a 10–0 crushing of helpless Second Division Hamilton Acas in the first leg of the League Cup quarter-final at Parkhead.

His second game was the Parkhead league fixture with Rangers, the third time the teams had met in less than two months, with two League Cup victories to Celtic.

But the script was changed for this one. True, Celtic had an extremely doubtful decision given against them when a Bobby Lennox equaliser was disallowed for offside when they were trailing 2–1.

It was a sad day for Celtic. Their manager, Jock Stein, was later rapped and fined by the S.F.A. for making remarks to a linesman at the end of the match.

Rangers won 4–2, and produced some of their best football for a long time, and at the end of the match the Frenchman puffed on his pipe and said. . . 'Our players can do as well as Rangers.'

Maybe even he was surprised at how near the truth he was to be proved.

Celtic flew out in warm autumn sunshine on the following Monday, anxious to shrug off the shattering impact which a defeat in an 'Old Firm' game can sometimes have on the losing team.

But there was a casualty list which did not make their task any easier. As well as Murdoch they left Tommy Gemmell at home, an injury victim from the previous Saturday.

Few Continental nations can resist the temptation to boost their prices for a European Cup game, and the French were no exception. They cashed in on Celtic's fame by simply doubling the admission charges for the 35,000 crowd, with a top price of £4.

The trim little St. Etienne ground had been improved in recent seasons, but the main stand still had an old-fashioned look about it . . . the air of a provincial club that seemed a little surprised to be in the front-line of a European campaign.

The banners and flags of the few hundred faithful fans who had flown over for the game welcomed the Celtic players as they trooped out of the team bus at the ground.

A heartening sight for players when they are abroad to see their own fans. But the same banners were soon drooping in near despair.

Celtic started the match as if they would disdainfully brush aside the French, but then slowly St. Etienne began to gain control.

And then in stepped a new star on the European stage . . . a thin, coloured inside-forward called Salif Keita.

St. Etienne moved swiftly on 'the break. Keita slammed in the first goal for the French after shots had been blocked from a free-kick, and in 37 minutes centre-forward Ravelli snapped a second in a goal-mouth mix-up after Ronnie Simpson seemed to have been impeded.

Celtic tried hard to get at least one goal back in the second-half, but their biggest worry came only minutes from the end.

Keita carved his way through the Celtic defence and fired a shot just past. That was dangerous enough, but a pass to his onrushing mates might have brought a third goal.

Stein stood in a somewhat quiet Celtic dressing-room and delivered a quick verdict. . . . 'We are still in, although we were lucky after our shocking first-half performance. But I have not given up hope.'

Unlike most British clubs, almost all the Continentals allow reporters and photographers to flood into their dressing-rooms after a match.

And it was a mob, as determined as any French rugby scrum, who swept in to crowd round a new European star in the home dressing-room.

Keita peeled off a sweat-stained green shirt, looked like Eusebio's kid brother, acknowledged all the congratulations, and said with magnificent simplicity:

'I do not want to be the new Eusebio or the new Pele. I am the first Keita.'

So Celtic faced again a one-round knock-out from the European Cup, an unenviable and unhappy position after the glory of Lisbon.

But one factor had got overlooked in that black week for Celtic – they lost to Rangers and St. Etienne and drew with Dunfermline – the players' own anger at their performance in France.

It was reflected as they sipped beers at the after-the-match banquet, it was the buzz of conversation as they flew home.

But most of all, it was reflected in ninety, heart-stopping minutes in the return game at Parkhead.

For me, this was the greatest of the six European Cup matches which capsuled so much triumph and tragedy.

I know thousands of fans will vote for the Red Star game at Parkhead, and that amazing score-line which finished with a 5-1 victory.

But I believe that any team who has to pull back a deficit, even if it is only one goal, has achieved one of the great peaks of modern soccer.

And that October night, by any standards, was a peak performance.

There had been a pre-match scare about an injured Celtic player, but it was not until the loudspeakers blared out the side that it was revealed it was Bobby Lennox who was missing.

Celtic started with typical fury, but Keita and his colleagues could be dangerous on the break, and it seemed their defence would at least hold out until the respite at half-time.

Then suddenly, far out on the right-wing, Joe McBride, making one of his last appearances in the big-time he relished before his transfer to Hibs, moved towards the goal, was fouled by left-back Camerini, and the referee gave a penalty.

If Britain had suddenly been allowed entry into the Common Market there could not have been a bigger fuss.

The angry French side crowded round Czech referee Zdenek Vales, they hurled lumps of mud to distract Tommy Gemmell as he waited to take the kick, they had to be shooed away from inside the arc round the penalty area.

Jock Stein confessed later that even for him the tension had been too much . . . he had been on his way up the tunnel to the dressing-room for half-time when the award was given, and had carried on.

The distractions might have put off any other player but Gemmell, the player whose self-confidence is never in doubt.

He stepped up, hammered the ball home, and there was no time even to centre the ball. It was a blow to the solar plexus for the French, the haven of the dressing-room which only minutes before had seemed so near now became an anxious discussion point about how they could hold on to their one-goal aggregate lead.

However, even that soon went, with a copy-book piece of over-lapping from Jim Craig, and just as everyone – forwards and defend-ers – lined up for the cross he slammed the ball into the net.

Chalmers was next to put them in the lead. It was at this point that

The perfect penalty kick . . . as Tommy Gemmell hammers the ball past St. Etienne 'keeper Garnus for his side's first goal against the French team.

Stein told me later: 'I suddenly realised that with away goals counting double, although we were leading 3–0, one snap goal from the French could still knock us out on aggregate.'

But his fears were soothed. Joe McBride got a fourth goal to seal one of the most memorable victories I have ever seen in the European Cup.

So there was no repeat of that chilling early exit from the European Cup of the previous season, and Celtic's name was back in the silver champagne bucket in the Geneva Hotel where the draw was made the next day.

This time it brought Celtic out against stern opposition, the rugged, no-nonsense Yugoslav Champions, Red Star of Belgrade.

A tough assignment. Name any of the Central European countries

It's ball juggling of a different kind . . . as Jimmy Johnstone shows his
skill with a golf club and ball before a game.

and they produce good top teams . . . physical sides, difficult to beat, always evenly balanced with robust players and skilful, scheming attackers.

But in the five weeks between the draw and the first match at Parkhead the paying customers were able to sit back, relax, and watch a side-show . . . the Jimmy Johnstone affair.

It started, like so many soccer storms, on the day when everyone who makes up the world of football – public, players, officials and Press – least expected it.

Celtic were cruising along on a 1–0 lead in a perfectly, ordinary league game against Dundee United at Parkhead . . . three days after the St. Etienne match.

Then with 12 minutes to go the signal from the home dug-out came for Johnstone to go off, and young George Connelly to take over as substitute.

Before Johnstone disappeared up the tunnel to the dressing-room, he stopped and seemed to say something to the officials in the dug-out. The fans who had taken their eyes off the field saw the amazing sight of manager Stein racing up after him.

The sequel was swift. At a board meeting just after the game, which Celtic won 2–0, the decision was taken to suspend the little right-winger for a week because of his behaviour to the club.

The sad little episode was tactfully cooled by Johnstone himself when he said the next day: 'It was a stupid thing to do and I have apologised.'

However, the next week he snapped back into the headlines when he told me: 'I do not want to play for Scotland.

'I would prefer at the moment to completely concentrate on Celtic. I feel I owe them that, after all that has happened.'

Eventually that, too, was smoothed over and Johnstone, the unpredictable genius of Parkhead, did play for Scotland in the next international, a World Cup qualifying game against Austria.

Stand by now, for episode three. The customers must have been as bewildered as I suppose Jimmy was at the way his name popped consistently into the headlines.

But episode three was the strangest of them all. For three days before the Red Star match manager Stein revealed in his Sunday newspaper column of the strange bargain he had struck with the little winger . . . because of Johnstone's fear of flying.

When Johnstone had gone to his manager before the game with the routine business of handing in his passport he had talked again about his dislike of travelling by plane.

It's not something new. He had made long tedious trips to Spain, once by car, once by train, to avoid flying even on holiday.

Stein told Jimmy that if Celtic won by 4-0 he could skip this trip with its long flights to and from the Yugoslav capital of Belgrade.

And in a bizarre twist nobody did more to earn that amazing 5-1 score-line for Celtic from the first game at Parkhead than wee Jimmy.

Certainly Celtic knew they had to get goals, but by the unwritten rules of the European competitions so does every team who play their first leg at home.

Stein had warned bluntly on the eve of the match: 'We need more than two goals. We need as many as we can possibly get. If we get two, I want to see us keep on scoring.'

Later he was to confess: 'I would have settled for a two-goal lead. I would have been over the moon with three. Now that Celtic are four ahead, I've caught a cold with shouting and can hardly speak.'

Yet at half-time on that November night, even the most fervent partisan Celtic fan in the 67,000 crowd could hardly have hoped for the final score.

Certainly it had looked at the start as if Celtic were going to cruise through the match. As the Red Star players anxiously tried to get the feel of the ground, adjust to the lung-bursting sound of the crowd and tiptoe their way through the first nervous minutes they found themselves in the position any team dreads in an away fixture in the European Cup.

They were a goal down. It had been executed quickly and brilliantly. A free-kick from Murdoch to Johnstone, the right-half ran on, got the ball back, and lashed the ball into the net, a copy-book tactical goal.

But slowly Red Star shrugged off the almost paralysing shock that goal had on them, gradually they began to show glimpses of the high quality of their ability.

Six minutes before half-time their come-back was completed when they equalised. Skipper Acimovic was their hero as he worked his way down the left, evaded tackles and crossed for centre Lazarevic to put the ball away from John Fallon, who was deputising for Ronnie Simpson injured playing for Scotland against Austria the week before.

The Yugoslavs were happy as they trooped off the Parkhead pitch at the interval. Away goals still counted double in this round, their 1-1 score was almost as good as a lead to them.

But all their hopes were to be blasted away in a wonderful spell at the start of the second-half by . . . well, I did say it was the Jimmy Johnstone show.

It's his biggest leap of the season, and the rare sight of little Jimmy Johnstone jumping up to challenge Raith Rovers 'keeper, Bobby Reid at Starks Park.

Like a boxer who has gone groggy to his corner at the end of a bad round, then been miraculously revived, Celtic raced out as if they had heard the bell sound.

Quickly the German referee, Herr Alfred Ott, gave a free-kick for Celtic after a foul on John Hughes. And when a defender failed to clear Johnstone stepped in to flash the ball into the net.

Red Star were down, not yet out, but the count had begun and the process was speeded up three minutes later when Johnstone crossed for his great buddy Bobby Lennox to score.

Willie Wallace scored a fourth and when just before the end Johnstone crowned possibly his greatest-ever Celtic performance with another wonderful goal, I don't believe the Parkhead fans would have swapped a pools win for such a second-half display.

The winger's amazing tally at the end of the game was two goals, and three assists. The off-the-field Johnstone who had made all these controversial stories, had been swept away on the best place for any footballer . . . on the park!

Still, he did not travel to Belgrade. Despite the fact that his manager wanted him to go, and some of his team-mates, possibly no keener on long trips, I suspect, thought he should have gone.

The Belgrade game was as great a contrast to the Parkhead match as two leg home and away ties can provide. Celtic did a cool, competent job to hold on to that lead, for even a four-goal start can suddenly appear dangerously thin if the opposition can pull back one or two quickly on their own ground.

The Yugoslav crowd who barely half-filled the still incomplete Maracana Stadium on a bitterly cold Belgrade afternoon, willed their side to try to get those goals.

But Celtic, controlled under pressure with a 4-3-3 formation, held on and when in 70 minutes Wallace substituted for Chalmers he celebrated by slamming his side into the lead.

For teams such as Celtic and Rangers, used to the support of massive fan fervour in every game, the effect of scoring a goal abroad must be a completely strange experience.

I remember watching Ronnie McKinnon head a last-minute aggregate equaliser for Rangers in the same stadium three years previously, to give them a play-off against Red Star.

The result was the same. Stunned and total silence, with far down from the heights of the press-box the only action off the field coming from manager Scot Symon, his training staff and reserves leaping up and down.

This time it was Jock Stein and his squad, and on the terracing a splash of green and white from the loyal, but few, Celtic fans in the 40,000 crowd who had journeyed across Europe to support their side.

Red Star did equalise in the closing minutes with a goal from Ostojic. I was impressed at the obvious annoyance the Celtic players showed even after the game about only drawing, although on the aggregate score it made only the slightest dent.

We flew home that night. Players, officials and press, and jetted back to Prestwick in less time than it takes to come by train from Aberdeen to Glasgow for a normal league fixture.

The thought was forming again in the players' minds, and their manager's, that the European Cup could again be brought back to Scotland.

Jock Stein said he would like to get Benfica, last season's finalists, in the quarter-finals, because they were an attacking team, but he had no strong preference.

However, the draw gave them Italian Champions, A.C. Milan . . . but that's another chapter!

Billy McNeill

My one position, almost without exception, since I bowed my way into the Celtic first team around ten years ago has been centre-half.

It's the position where simply you are there to stop goals being scored, not to get your own name on the score-sheet.

That's why every time I look at a list of scorers and see the name McNeill I still wonder a bit about it all.

When I started in First Division football everyone was liable to think a centre-half had gone out of his mind if he put a foot over the half-way line.

The start of the change for me came one March afternoon in 1961. It was completely unrehearsed, a move which sprang from a half-time chat in the dressing-room.

Celtic were playing Ayr United at Somerset Park, and we were trailing 1–0. I remember sitting talking to two of my team-mates, Pat Crerand and Bertie Peacock.

I said then that if I saw a chance I was going to nip upfield and see if I could take advantage of it. Maybe they put it down to a centre-half wanting to play centre-forward, but no one tried to change my mind.

And soon after the interval, I saw my chance and grabbed the equaliser, then we went on to win 3–1.

However I must admit it was not a regular tactic until manager Jock Stein joined the club in 1965. He instructed me to move up at corner-kicks and try to use my height to advantage.

It almost came off in the Scottish Cup semi-final against Motherwell when I hit the post, but what a wonderful pay-off in the Cup Final that year.

Remember it was eleven years since Celtic had won the Scottish Cup, eight years since we had won any major honour.

I look back along all the honours we have won in recent seasons, and they have all had wonderful moments, but that 1965 Cup Final has a special place in my memory.

We were playing manager Stein's old team, Dunfermline, and we had a score to settle with them for they had beaten us in the Final of 1961.

It was a terrific struggle. Twice they went ahead, and twice Celtic equalised. Then fifteen minutes from time I managed to get my head to a Charlie Gallagher cross and nod it into the net.

Since then it has become a set part of our tactics. Even if I don't get to every corner I am still making room for our forwards to take advantage.

There have been some magic moments for me such as the goal which gave us a 1-0 victory in the World Championship match against Racing Club at Hampden.

The first goal against Rangers in the Scottish Cup Final, and of course, the last-minute winner against Vojvodina in the European Cup.

I think that's the one I would place above them all. Vojvodina were one of the best sides we have ever met in Europe, and it looked as if we would need a play-off to decide the winner of the quarter-final tie.

That was the season Celtic won the European Cup. We had lost 1-0 in Yugoslavia, but Steve Chalmers had equalised for us in the second-half at Parkhead.

The crowd had encouraged us, we had battled at that Vojvodina defence but we just couldn't get the ball past them.

The signal had come from the dug-out that there was only minutes to go, when Charlie Gallagher took a corner on the right and I was lucky enough to head it into the net.

What a marvellous moment. Not only had we won, it saved us from the fixture chaos of a third game at a time when we were still chasing the league championship, and the Scottish cup, both of which we won.

Don't believe it is easy in that penalty area. There is more jostling going on than anyone on the terracing can possibly see.

I believe defenders dislike other defenders going up into the attack more than anything else. They have it in for them with harder

The slog behind the headline goals. Billy McNeill hammers at the ball in
a training session, part of his campaign which has paid off so often with
so many great goals.

treatment than they ever give to forwards.

Maybe these goals go some way to make up for the one that was scored against me last season, when A.C. Milan knocked Celtic out of the European Cup at Parkhead.

The goal was scored in the twelfth minute by Piero Prati, because I fumbled a throw-in from Jim Craig in a position from which apparently there was no danger.

I can offer no excuses. As a professional I should not have made the mistake, the worst moment of my senior career.

Why did it happen? Believe me, I have run that move through the film of my memory hundreds of times since that March night.

If I had played the ball first time I'd have been all right. But I wanted to do something useful with it. It bounced off my shin as I tried to collect it.

Even then I might have got away with it if I had just tried to block Prati. But I tried to poke the ball to John Clark. Prati nipped away and that was that.

It was a move I have made thousands of times. I can only describe the mistake as similar to the error a car driver might make after years of safe driving.

Fortunately we went on to win the league championship again, and yet another chance in the European Cup.

I believe it is the European tournaments which are the real test for Celtic now. Any team needs to be stretched, and it is in these tournaments we could reach our full potential.

Don't get me wrong. I am not writing off the Scottish tournaments. These are the passport to Europe, and at the top level I believe there has been an improvement in Scottish soccer.

But, to be honest, there are still too many teams who if they even draw with ourselves or Rangers it is a seven-day sensation.

There can be no letting up for us on the domestic front. We have already won four championships in succession, we are anxious to go ahead and equal the record of six in a row set up by a Celtic side at the beginning of the century.

I think that the improvement in the general standard is greatly due to Celtic. Our style of soccer in recent seasons has been shown to be the one the fans wanted to see.

It brought a freedom of expression in tactics which helped to change a string of ideas on football.

The difference in football from even ten years ago is fantastic. Take one position, full-back. It used to be the least glamorous job on the park.

Another leap by Billy McNeill . . . another life-saver for Celtic. This time the centre-half (*nearest the post*) was leaping up to head Celtic's equaliser against Hibs at Easter Road, a game they powered on to win 5–2.

Full-backs were expected to do only two things, scare the wingers and belt the ball up the park.

Now if a full-back cannot find time to move up the park and overlap with his winger everyone rates him as old-fashioned.

One player who was well ahead of his time in his thinking on the full-back position was Duncan MacKay, who played with me when I first went into the Celtic league side.

He had all the ideas about overlapping, and joining in the attack. But nobody wanted to know at that time. Still, a great player.

However most of all, there has been the change in the status of footballers. I gave up a good job to become a full-time footballer. Some people wondered about it, footballers were all supposed to be brainless.

That sort of sneer has been wiped out to a great extent now. Not every footballer's brains are in his feet. It is recognised now more as a career from which there can be a great deal of reward to kids who are prepared to give it the proper amount of work.

Not all of them perhaps can reach the heights of some of the great players I have opposed, but they can make a very good living.

The four top players in my soccer span were Masopust of Czechoslovakia, Di Stefano, Bobby Charlton and Jim Baxter.

Masopust played against Scotland in a World Cup game in Brati-

It looks a perfect goal, Billy McNeill jumps up in triumph as the ball enters the net, and Bobby Lennox turns to congratulate his captain. But this time the goal, which would have given a last minute victory against Airdrie at Parkhead, was disallowed.

slava in 1961, and it was a soccer education just to watch him.

He still showed signs of his greatness six years later when he was a veteran and played for Dukla Prague against Celtic in the European Cup semi-final.

Di Stefano was still a Real Madrid star when they beat us 3–1 in a charity friendly match at Parkhead in 1962.

Maybe that one match sums up the difference between then and now with Celtic. After the match the crowd chanted for us to do a lap of honour . . . I think they were so pleased we had not been crushed.

It was then that we realised, maybe more than at any time, just how much they wanted us to win something.

Now if we were beaten 3–1 by Real Madrid at home there would be a full-scale inquest.

Charlton is one of the world's greatest players, for he has made the move back from striker to mid-field and been successful in both of them. I know from playing against him at Wembley last season, just how difficult he can be to pin down.

Right up with the best of them in his glory days for Rangers was Jim Baxter. I played with him in Scotland's international sides, and I played against him in 'Old Firm' matches.

He was one of the greatest mid-field players I have ever seen, a

43

man who could inspire a team by his sheer soccer ability, and touch of arrogance.

Jim would try to talk you off a game, even although he and I were good friends off the park.

These were the days when he was in a Rangers side picking up most of the honours, and Celtic were waiting down below to pick up the losers' medals.

I know what it's like. It's not even so bad if you lose in a semi-final of a Cup. Nobody can ever tell you two months after it who were the two defeated semi-finalists.

It's traditional you should take the Cup into the losers' dressing-room, but I feel it's only rubbing the defeat in. I know I felt that way when I took the League Cup into the Hibs dressing-room after the final last season.

What about my future? I'm not ready to pack in the playing side of football, not for a long time yet.

But I am often asked if I will eventually become a manager. I can only say that at the moment the idea does not appeal to me too much. However I would like to stay in football in some way. . . . I hope it's a problem I don't have to face for a good few seasons yet.

Willie Wallace

The day I signed for Celtic I posed for a picture in the dressing-room in front of the number 7, 8, 9 and 10 strips.

I never realised I was going to use them all!

Still, I have no complaints about where I am fielded. After all, I finished last season as Celtic's leading goal-scorer, so it shows that switching around does not affect my play.

When I started with Stenhousemuir, my first senior club, I was outside-right, an old-fashioned winger with sawdust on my boots.

Then when I moved to Raith Rovers it was Bert Herdman who was then their manager, who moved me to centre.

And I have shuffled around the three inside-forward positions ever since. Frankly in modern football I don't think the numbers game means very much.

At Parkhead we usually play with two front-runners, Bobby Lennox, Steve Chalmers or myself, for our forward line is constantly changed by the manager.

I think that is one of the secrets of the Celtic success. As recently as ten years ago when a team hit a successful run that was the way it stayed . . . until someone was injured.

No one was changed. The same formation was played, but our system is different. Almost every week there is some change in the line-up or some change in tactics to baffle the opposition.

I did have a spell last season playing slightly deeper. I had started off the season scoring very well, but I then lost my touch.

So Mr. Stein told me to play back a little. I knew I was not playing well at the time, and I was grateful for not being dropped. That is

45

also a secret of the Celtic success – like all club teams – a player is not axed after one or two bad games.

He might be rested, or he might be switched to a new role. It certainly worked for me when I found my scoring boots again.

I have also had a spell in mid-field, especially two seasons ago. I had a bit of success there at the time, but I honestly don't feel it is my best position. I think it was just a case of a change working well at the time.

My way to Celtic was slightly different from most of the rest of the team, who had gone direct to the club as teenagers.

I had worked my way through Stenhousemuir, Raith Rovers and then Hearts before I was transferred in November 1966.

My first club was the junior Kilsyth Rangers. I hope it does not make me sound like a soccer greybeard, but I regret the change in the world of junior football.

Then as mere teenagers we played against teams packed with veterans who knew every dodge of the game. I picked up a lot of vital experience which otherwise I would have missed.

Now the emphasis is all on teenagers, and the seniors do not regard the juniors as the most important nursery sides, but I feel it's a pity.

When I moved to Raith Rovers I played in a team sprinkled with famous names such as Willie McNaught – and what a help he was to me in my career – and Jim Baxter.

That was before he moved to Rangers and stardom. He used to drive up to training on a motor-cycle and wearing a T-shirt.

But even then you could glimpse all his football class. He usually played inside-left, I remember being amazed one day – and so were the Motherwell defence – at a game at Fir Park when he swerved past at least six players on a run from the bye-line to score.

He was even in a team which beat Rangers at Ibrox. Raith won 3–2, after they had been two goals down in the first ten minutes.

When I moved to Hearts it was also into a new world of European football. Hearts had been in the European Cup, and they were constantly in the Fairs Cup.

We played top teams such as Inter-Milan – when Helenio Herrera had just been taken over, and that time anyway I was on the losing side.

My troubles with Hearts, which eventually ended with my move to Celtic, began around 1965, over the question of a benefit, and when I was left out a close-season tour to Norway because I had refused to re-sign.

46

Goal-scoring made simple . . . as Willie Wallace keeps his eye firmly on the ball before putting it into the Rangers net for his second goal against Rangers at Ibrox in the League Cup.

Eventually, after I had put in a number of transfer requests, and they had all been refused, manager Tommy Walker left the club, and John Harvey, who was then the trainer, took over.

Mr. Harvey asked me if I wanted to stay, but I had made up my mind to leave, and soon after I was transferred to Celtic.

The agony and the ecstasy of an 'Old Firm' goal. The men with defeat mirrored on their faces are Rangers defenders John Greig and Norrie Martin. The man in the human victory sign is outside-right Jimmy Johnstone as his team-mates in the background rush to congratulate scorer Willie Wallace after his first goal in the League Cup against Rangers at Ibrox.

I was told later that one Hearts official said I could move because they thought I would be no use to Celtic!

You can imagine how that made me want to show them just how wrong they were.

My biggest disappointment at Hearts was our failure to win the League Championship in 1965, when we only needed to draw with Kilmarnock at Tynecastle.

I think that match showed the difference between the old and modern ways of football. We went out into that vital match with no plan, just a collection of eleven individual units hoping for a win.

It's history now that we lost 2–0, and lost the league!

Such a situation could never happen at Parkhead. I don't mean that we are over-planned, I don't mean that we never lose games. But at least a reasonable amount of work is put into our games.

The difference in playing for Celtic shows itself in a hundred ways. But one of the main ones is the encouragement from the crowds.

Everywhere we play our fans are there. During the years I was at

Seven, eight, nine, or ten? It's the four positions of Willie Wallace as he holds up a Celtic jersey on the night he signed for them from Hearts.

Tynecastle the games were dropping steadily from around 15,000 to 7,000.

I soon found out just how much the crowd meant to Celtic. Because of the European Cup registration regulations I missed the quarter-final tie against Vojvodina – a team I rated at the time as one of the best defensive sides in Europe.

But, even sitting in the stand, I could sense the encouragement the crowd gave the team which was climaxed by that last seconds winning goal by Billy McNeill.

And I made a scoring debut when I finally did play against Dukla Prague in the semi-final, with two goals in a 3–1 victory.

The one which pleased me most was the third one, from a Bertie Auld free-kick, a move we had often practised at training. There is a great deal of satisfaction about scoring a goal over which there has been planning.

For any Celtic player who was in the European Cup victory against Inter-Milan that must be the highlight of his career.

But, of course, there have been a succession of honours, and everyone has his own individual favourite.

Mine was the 1967 Cup Final – the year we won all the honours – when we beat Aberdeen 2–0, and I scored both the goals.

It is a thrill for any player to score in a Cup Final. But mine had a particular tang of pleasure. Most of my team-mates had been in Cup Finals, some of them in the winning 1965 side.

I had never previously been in a team which had gone beyond the second-round!

And last season I had another Cup-winners medal to join it, after the victory against Rangers!

I have played in both Scotland's great derby games, Celtic and Rangers and Hearts against Hibs.

They really cannot be compared. Generally there is more football from both teams in the East of Scotland derby.

I would not say for a moment that there is no skill in the 'Old Firm' games. I think Celtic showed that in the Cup Final.

But from the matches I have been in between Celtic and Rangers it is rare for both sides to hit a good game in the same match. The tension from the terracing too often stifles any real soccer.

And in the Edinburgh derby game no one goes in fear that if they make one false pass it will bring about jeering from the opposing fans.

I don't know what they are like right now, but certainly when I played we had some great games with Hibs. I can remember one 5–3 victory, for Hearts.

My first experience with the international team was when I was still with Hearts, and since I moved to Celtic I have been included in the Scottish team pool.

I certainly would love to help Scotland win through to Mexico. But if we fail to qualify I reckon team boss Bobby Brown should try an entirely new policy.

He should start again with a team of players, all of them Under-23. That would mean scrapping a lot of players . . . including myself!

Sure they would have bad results, but by the end of the experiment they would all only be in their middle twenties, and I think they would have achieved a proper blend.

It is no use keeping on players getting towards their late twenties, most of them will be no good for the 1974 World Cup.

It would be a drastic method, but if we have another World Cup flop on top of our previous failures I feel it would be worth a try.

League Cup

How do you like your Cup Finals? Served piping hot with tension exploding like November fireworks, or cooler with the emphasis on elegance and soccer skills?

Football fans had the chance to compare the two styles in a vivid contrast between the Scottish Cup Final, involving, of course, Celtic and Rangers and the League Cup Final between Celtic and Hibs.

There is no match like an 'Old Firm' game for tension wrapping itself around a game, the reason why so few of them ever turn into memorable football spectacles.

By a fixture freak the two Cup Finals were played in the space of three weeks, instead of being separated by five months.

Away back in October the Celtic team had been at their Cup headquarters at Seamill preparing for the match against Hibs when they heard that the Hampden stand had been damaged by fire.

The game was postponed, and it was April before a gap could be found in the crowded fixture list to fit in one of the season's three main trophies.

. It was a day to make you glad they had arranged to play a Cup Final. It was Easter week-end, and one of the few occasions in a bleak spring when the weather relented.

The wind and rain which so mercilessly whipped its way through March, April and even May, took time off, and helped boost the crowd to 74,000.

The weather was not the only reason for such a box-office boost. The teams had met two weeks before the final in a 1–1 draw in a

Moment of triumph . . . for Bertie Auld as he holds the League Cup and shows it to the crowd after the victory against Hibs at Hampden.

league match at Parkhead, a shock point dropped by Celtic.

And perhaps, also, the fans' memories stretched back to a marvellous 5–2 league victory for Celtic at Easter Road earlier in the season.

The League Cup had been on the Parkhead sideboard for three seasons, with two victories against Rangers and one against Dundee in the previous finals.

Celtic had suffered a severe blow when John Hughes, possibly then at the peak of his form for the season, was injured in a League game against St. Johnstone at Perth four days before the final.

It was an injury which was to rule him out of football for the entire month of April, the crucial time when so many of the season's honours are settled.

So the Celtic side to defend the trophy, which had become almost a part of the Parkhead furniture, lined up: Fallon; Craig, Gemmell; Murdoch, McNeill, Brogan; Johnstone, Lennox, Chalmers, Wallace, Auld, with John Clark as substitute.

And Hibs side was Allan; Shevlane, Davis; Stanton, Madsen, Blackley; Marinello, Quinn, Cormack, O'Rourke, Stevenson, with Hunter as twelfth man.

53

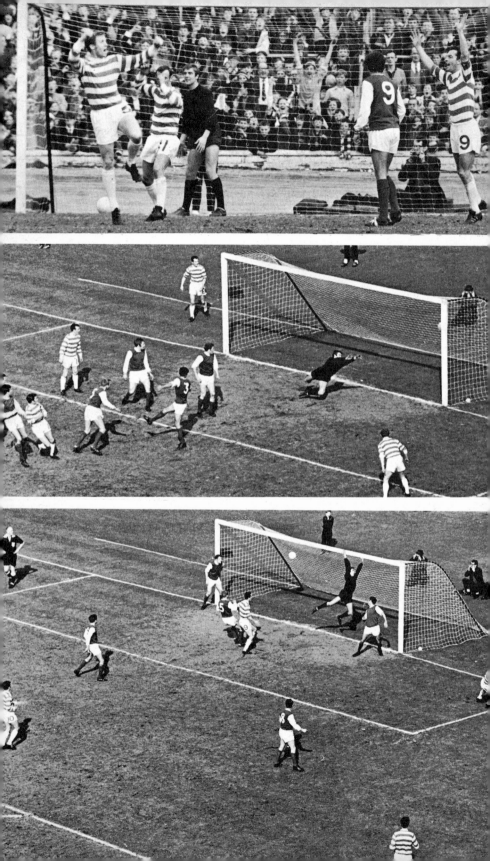

This was Hampden at its best, bathed in spring sunshine, ready to provide a football festival.

And after 15 minutes of mid-field deadlock as both teams probed to find gaps – with a Bobby Murdoch shot going past and Eric Stevenson missing a great chance for Hibs – the goal parade started up.

Number one was in 28 minutes. Bertie Auld swung over a free-kick from the right. As always Billy McNeill was up to aid his forwards at such a move, and the ball broke off from him and a Hibs defender to Willie Wallace who slammed it through a crowded goalmouth into the net.

Number two came four minutes later as Hibs nervously tried to regroup their players. And, like some of the others which were to add style to this final, the move could have come out of a football text-book.

A ball was swung down the left between Auld, Lennox and Steve Chalmers and it was the left-winger who finished off the move by hitting the ball high into the net.

Number three came at that most vital of times, a minute before the interval, a k.o. header from Bobby Lennox after a Johnstone corner.

Number four was in 58 minutes, a perfect Auld pass from midfield was slotted on to Lennox to score.

Number five was in 75 minutes, to give Lennox his hat-trick after a Chalmers run.

Number six came a minute later when the bewildered Hibs defence were caught out after right-back Jim Craig had slammed in a rebound from a cross which had been blocked.

That finished the Celtic scoring spree, a brilliant exhibition of attacking football which has made them famous at its best.

John Clark came on as substitute for Tommy Gemmell, and not even two late lapses inside the last ten minutes when Jim O'Rourke and Stevenson scored could wipe the gloss off the Celtic victory.

It was the perfect blast-off for their April march to Scotland's honours, and their task in the league championship was eased considerably that day.

Celtic's first goal . . . and the delighted Parkhead line-up is, *left to right*, Billy McNeill, Bobby Lennox, and Steve Chalmers after a shot from Willie Wallace, not in picture, has gone into the net.

He's just in the picture, but the ball's in the net all the same, as Bertie Auld, third from left, slams his shot past a crowd of Hibs defenders for Celtic's second goal

It looks as if he's facing the wrong way. But it's just Bobby Lennox, *extreme right*, wheeling away from the Hibs goal as the ball beats Hibs 'keeper Allan for the third goal.

For, as the thousands of Celtic fans cheered their team as they were presented with the Cup, the news flashed round the Hampden terracing that Rangers had been beaten by Dundee United at Tannadice.

I reckon the cheer that greeted that result was just as great as the one for the Cup presentation.

It meant that Celtic had virtually won two trophies in one afternoon . . . and no team can do much better than that.

It had been a sunshine soccer occasion, but I wonder how many of the fans cast their minds back to the game which had started it all, the first of the season against Rangers at Ibrox.

The two teams had been drawn together in the same section of the League Cup, along with Partick Thistle and Morton.

The biggest crowd of the day in Britain, 80,000 fans, packed into Ibrox for the match, and when it finished with a 2–0 victory for Celtic the bookies' odds on Celtic winning the treble of Scottish trophies had tumbled to 9–2 . . . they were not such bad judges either.

The man who ran up that 2–0 score-line was centre-forward Willie Wallace, one of the most consistent of the Celtic forwards throughout the season.

But it was a personal disaster for Rangers skipper John Greig, who twice cracked in the first-half as both teams battled to get the vital first goal.

The first slip came in nine minutes when a ball from young George Connelly – he was making his league debut – bounced away from Greig.

Johnstone, who was listed at inside-right, sped through and the ball spun off 'keeper Martin for Wallace to slam it in.

Then in 36 minutes came another Rangers defensive blunder. Bobby Lennox harried Greig out on the right-wing and the Ranger tried to turn the ball back to Martin.

However, he clipped it across to Wallace who snapped on it like a soccer baracuda and shot the ball into the net.

That was the points wrapped up, Rangers failed to stage an effective come-back, and Celtic looked favourites to beat their biggest rivals in the qualifying race.

Two weeks later in the return match at Parkhead it was Wallace again. This time he had to wait until the seventy-fifth minute before he scored.

Congratulations from Bobby Murdoch, Steve Chalmers and Jimmy Johnstone to the man in the middle . . . Bobby Lennox after he scored Celtic's fourth goal, and his own second.

It's one between three, but Bobby Lennox makes no mistake as he snatches his own hat-trick, and Celtic's fifth goal . . . and there's nothing defenders Joe Davis, Thomson Allan and Chris Shevlane can do about it.

The final thrust from Celtic, and this time it's full-back Jim Craig who gets in the scoring act as, *third from left*, he watches his shot speed into goal.

It was John Hughes who made the goal, with a thundering shot from 20 yards to break the scoring deadlock.

'Keeper Martin amazingly managed to touch it onto the bar, it spun down to a trio of waiting Celtic forwards and Wallace scored.

That took Wallace's goal tally to eight in four games . . . nice start of the season scoring!

Near the end of that match Tommy Gemmell missed a penalty after a Mathieson tackle on Wallace.

That virtually wrapped up the section for Celtic, whose fans waited behind at the end to chant 'We'll be running round Hampden with the Cup.'

Still, it had been a fierce encounter before the 70,000 all-ticket crowd. Three players had been booked in the first 15 minutes, John Hughes and Bobby Murdoch of Celtic and Rangers inside-right Alex Ferguson.

Celtic won the other matches in the section, 4–1 against Morton at Parkhead, and 3–0 at Greenock and 4–0 against Partick Thistle at Parkhead and 6–1 at Firhill.

Then came the Second Division lambs for the slaughter in the quarter-finals, a 10–0 crushing of Second Division Hamilton Acas at Parkhead.

Too cruel a score? The allegation was made, but I don't think it stands up. Remember that it was a quarter-final of a national competition, both teams had won their places on merit.

Celtic would have been foolish, with a tightly-packed fixture list, to have ignored the chance to really finish the tie in one game.

They were able to play the second game at Douglas Park and field a team well sprinkled with reserves . . . and still win 4–2.

They had a somewhat shaky semi-final against Clyde at Hampden, with a 77-minute winner from George Connelly to get through 1–0.

It was his first Hampden appearance, and five months later on his second match on Scotland's biggest ground he was to score another vital goal.

So they moved to the wait-for-it final . . . and it was worth the delay. Poor Hibs really did not have a chance. Perhaps if they could have scored the first goal, perhaps if they could have stopped the scoring flow at two until half-time.

But you could write a book on the ifs of football alone. It was a memorable final, touched with the jewels of some great goals . . . and it was to be a memorable month.

John Hughes

This is the age of the teenager. It's the time when fresh-faced seventeen year olds can shoot to overnight fame, whether their world is football, or pop records.

I wish them all luck. But at the ripe old age of 26 I can honestly say . . . they're welcome to it.

I've been through it all before. The adulation, the brickbats, the teenage wonder tag, and a few other names as well, most of them unprintable.

For after nine seasons in Celtic's league side it's only in the last two years that I consider myself a fully qualified professional.

Let me take you back to 1960. That was when the Hughes and Celtic story began. Maybe now it had the wrong kind of start . . . it was too good.

I was only seventeen, my first season at Parkhead, and after only two weeks I was playing against Rangers in a League Cup match at Ibrox.

Any Celtic player will tell you he always gets pleasure out of scoring against Rangers, and I know it is the same for the Ibrox players when they score against us.

Well, I started with the kind of debut which should really belong to boys' comics. I was playing against Doug Baillie, newly signed from Airdrie and making his Ibrox debut.

Remember this was in the era before the Rangers' big buys. A newly-signed player was still a comparative rarity for them, and it added extra spice to a game which is never short of that.

It was the battle of the newcomers, and the customers relished the clash.

It turned out to be a glory day for me, and a disaster for Doug, who had been a solid, reliable player for the Broomfield club.

It was topped off for me when I scored the winning goal, we won the match 3–2, and after that poor Doug never really established himself in all his time at Ibrox.

The wrong kind of start for me. It did not seem so then. I was hailed as the new superstar, the boy who was going to change Celtic.

It was ridiculous, of course. But remember these were the lean years for Celtic. It had been three years since their last trophy success, the 7–1 League Cup victory against Rangers.

But you can't live for ever on the memory of one trophy win if your main rivals are busily scooping up the current awards.

Celtic fans were desperate for a success, they were desperate for some new name to chant around the football parks of Scotland.

That day at Ibrox it seemed to them they had got one. I could do no wrong . . . for a time at any rate.

But it did not last. A few months later I was being rested, and for almost five years that was the tale of my soccer life.

In, out, in, out. I was big, awkward . . . and I knew it. Because of my height there was no way I could hide on that park, every move I made stood out, even in the middle of a ruck of players I towered over most of them.

When I scored five goals in an 8–0 victory against Aberdeen a Celtic official was quoted as saying: 'Hughes was in top form,' and then he added carefully: 'It's to be hoped he can keep it up.'

That was the tale of my soccer life. Consistency, the most vital ingredient for any team or any player was lacking.

The fans who cheered me, just as often booed me. One day at Stirling I fell onto the track as I was going for a ball.

I looked up from the track of that tight little Annfield ground, and recognised out of the sea of faces shouting abuse at me, one man I knew.

He turned out to be a person for whom I often got complimentary tickets for games. Needless to say, he did not get any more, but I began to feel I just couldn't win.

But the worst moment of my soccer career came from a team-mate. He's an international star, now with a top English club, but in my hearing he told our coach Sean Fallon, that if I was included in the team he would not play.

It was the cruellest remark I have ever heard. You can imagine

Eye on the ball, arm outstretched for balance . . . and it's John Hughes
poised to shoot at a Scottish team training session.

The worst moment of the season . . . for John Hughes as a conference with manager Stein and trainer Mochan on the eve of the Cup Final rules him out of the match.

what effect it had on my confidence. I reckon now it set me back almost two seasons..

I hope I would never hear such a remark made about any youngster when I'm around.

Maybe if I had been given better advice earlier in my career I would have made the break-through quicker.

But it took the greatest moment in Celtic's history to make me realise I had to improve my form by all-out effort . . . or make a move to another club.

It was the 1967 European Cup Final against Inter-Milan in Lisbon,

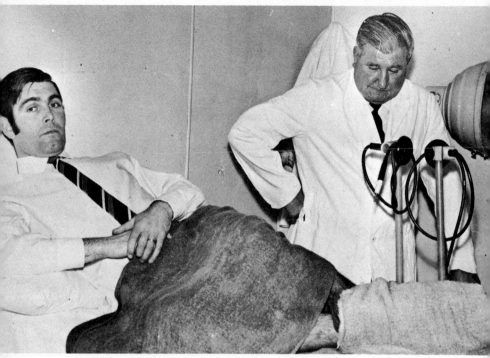

Sadly a too familiar scene for John Hughes during the last month of the season . . . as he received treatment from physiotherapist Bob Rooney.

and the Celtic forward line read Johnstone, Wallace, Chalmers, Auld and Lennox . . . but no John Hughes.

I had been injured. But secretly I suspected that even if I had been available I might not have been in the team.

I knew then how Jimmy Greaves must have felt the season before when Sir Alf Ramsey left him out of the World Cup Final side.

Of course, I was delighted that Celtic had won, I am a Celtic player. But I couldn't help thinking how I would have loved to have been on that field helping them to win it.

The only person who could change things was myself. The first step was to slog away at a diet.

I admit it, I like my food. But some of my favourite dishes were ruled out in the battle of the bulge, and it was worth it.

Now I still watch my weight, but I am not on a strict diet, it is everything in moderation.

Once you have touched success at the top, once you have found moves which have been planned working out successfully, once you have confidence . . . then you don't want to go back to the old ways.

I realise there will be times when my form will slip, I think it's impossible for any player not to suffer occasionally from that.

But I will never go back permanently to the image of the old John Hughes. That has disappeared for ever . . . I'm sure about that.

It may surprise some people that I have named last season as one of my most successful. For after a tackle in the game against St. Johnstone my ankle was damaged, and I missed the entire month of April . . . the League Cup Final, then the Scottish Cup Final, and the last few games in the League championship.

Naturally I was disappointed, especially at being out of the Scottish Cup Final.

However I think I proved right up until my injury that my form had been more consistent perhaps than any other season.

It had been a season in which I had taken a lot of knocks. Some of them were fair, others were not. But I have learned now that I am going to have to take them, and get on with my job.

Perhaps the best boost to my form has been confidence. One goal perhaps summed it up, against St. Mirren at Love Street.

Jim Brogan shoved through a ball, I went after it, beat a defender and then the onrushing 'keeper Jim Thorburn to score. It's the kind of shot which only a few seasons ago it's odds on I would have fumbled.

My biggest disappointment last season was our failure in the European Cup Final, when we lost to A.C. Milan in the quarter-final.

I have one ambition above any others in football. I want a European Cup-Winners medal . . . and I am sure it will come yet.

For me, there is nothing like these European Cup matches. They are the fizz on the football champagne.

Our policy is to win matches, and just as important to entertain, at all times. The domestic matches are the bread and butter which pave the way into Europe . . . and the manager never lets us forget it.

Yet I think Europe is still the greatest test of our potential. At the very top there are no favourites. Unlike some of our Scottish matches when it is considered a formality for us to win.

The slightest break one way or another can mean victory, as Milan showed against us at Parkhead.

It's always fascinating to compare teams we played against before the Celtic break-through, to consider how they would manage against the present Parkhead team.

Of course, it is an impossibility. But the one game I often think about would be against the Rangers team of the early sixties . . . the

65

Ibrox era of Ian McMillan and Jim Baxter.

Baxter is the player I remember most from these games. Supremely arrogant, but most of all the man whom all the other Rangers players used to look for when they were in trouble . . . and the man who was always there.

It's a great pity that the gulf between the fans of the two clubs seems bigger than ever.

Personally 'Old Firm' matches are not ones I enjoy, for I feel that the chances of both teams hitting top form with the background of the fierce terracing battles are too rare.

And I am sorry to see – or should I say, hear – the rivalry carried into Scotland's international team.

These chants from Rangers fans at international matches for their own players are just about the cruellest I have ever heard in sport.

What do they want? Eleven Rangers players on the field. They might get their wish in the end. I can't see players from other clubs, and not just Celtic, going out to try their best and then receiving terracing abuse.

Maybe it's just as well our remaining World Cup matches are away from home . . . at least it should free us from those terracing barrackings.

If Scotland is ever going to get anywhere as a world power at international level, and not just club level, it means everyone has to play their part . . . and that means the fans just as much as the players!

Scottish Cup Final

If you were presented with the choice of a match ticket for any game in the world it is the one on your own doorstep, which, from all the panorama of soccer, could still provide a scene different from any other.

Take the finish of an 'Old Firm' match, especially if the score-line has swung decisively for one team.

At one end of the ground the fans are packed in solid ranks, not a single slit of terracing showing, as they chant their joy to the gods of sport.

At the other end of the strictly segregated terracing, shrouded in the special brand of misery which defeat in these matches can produce, a few hundred fans winding to the exits, the remnants of an army of thousands who have long since left the battle.

It is as traditional as Hogmanay hangovers, as predictable as the seasons, it is the one factor in football which never changes.

If you had been hovering in a helicopter just above Hampden at around 4.40 p.m. on Saturday 26 April, you would have looked down on such an amazing soccer scene – all the joy and agony of victor and defeated capsuled into the two ends of the ground.

There is no lap of honour allowed at Hampden after a Cup Final. The highlight of Wembley – even if TV interviewers spoiled it this year – when the fans pay homage to their team is banned in Scotland.

And at the final whistle when a fan dashed from the Rangers end and did one of the fastest sprints of the day down the field – dropping a bottle on the way – and into the arms of a waiting guard of police-

George Connelly runs forward to the Celtic end after he had scored their third goal.

men it showed that no lap of honour is a sensible decision, at least for an 'Old Firm' final.

So it is up to the fans to find an equivalent way of honouring their heroes. And this time they did it with their voices.

As Skipper Billy McNeill received the Cup he held it high to show it to the fans, and then instead of clutching on to it he passed it back so that each succeeding player also lifted it above his head to wave it to the fans.

It brought eleven separate roars from the Celtic fans, a crowd of 50,000 wrapped as if they were one man in a special brand of ecstasy.

It had been a memorable victory. The score-line read Celtic 4, Rangers 0 . . . the day the football record book had been re-written.

For in the terms of statistics it was a record-winning twentieth Cup Final victory for Celtic, their first against Rangers in a final since 1904, and Rangers first defeat from any side in a Cup Final since 1930.

The background to the match, as the two giants moved slowly through the earlier rounds and apparently inevitably to the final clash, had taken up more space than a string of Cup Finals would usually collect.

It had spilled from the sports pages of the press on to the news side as first came the Colin Stein ordering-off and suspension which had ruled him out of the Rangers side . . . and you would need a whole book on its own to describe that story.

Five days before the final at an S.F.A. Referee Committee meeting Celtic had lost Jimmy Johnstone, suspended after his third caution of the season against St. Johnstone.

It seemed that the scales of soccer justice were going to be finely balanced, a star player missing from each side.

Then on the Friday morning at a final training session on the lush lawn beside the hotel headquarters at Troon came what seemed a crushing blow.

John Hughes, whose fitness battle for the previous three weeks after an injury against St. Johnstone, had been followed with the closeness of a serial story, was finally ruled out of the game he wanted so much – and had worked so hard – to play in.

The bookies could not split either team. It was the game where most of the tipsters predicted a draw, because from long and bitter experience you learn that only palmists and crystal-gazers would hazard a forecast on these matches.

And in less than two minutes Celtic showed why these games still retain the tag of the most unpredictable in the country.

The teams had lined up: Celtic: Fallon; Craig, Gemmell;

Murdoch, McNeill, Brogan, Connelly, Chalmers, Wallace, Lennox, Auld, with John Clark as substitute.

Rangers: Martin; Johansen, Mathieson; Greig, McKinnon, D. Smith; Henderson, Penman, Ferguson, Johnston, Persson, and Jardine as substitute.

For in that second minute Celtic struck, with the oldest and still one of the most deadly attacking methods in football . . . the high corner-kick, the header bulleted into the net.

The danger started when Rangers centre-half Ronnie McKinnon conceded a corner down at the east end corner of the park.

Little Bobby Lennox swung over the ball, and as so often centre-half Billy McNeill was up in an attacking role at a corner to arc the ball into the net off the base of the post.

If McNeill had touched the depths of soccer misery against Milan that one moment must have made it all up for him.

Yet so often there is a possee of defenders around him. For some unknown reason this time there was no one.

He stood completely isolated, and all the astonished Ibrox defenders could do was to stand and point at each other.

The marking had collapsed, and at a vital period of the game. Celtic officials claimed later that they were not surprised at such an early goal, but I suspect they were saying it with their tongues slightly in their cheeks.

No planners could possibly budget for such a shot of adrenalin being pumped into their team so quickly.

Rangers had walked on to Hampden with the conviction that their three-year spell without honours was ending.

They had planned to open the gates of Ibrox to let the crowd in to see the Cup if they had won it. . . .

The gates must have been gently pushed shut when the news of that goal was flashed to them.

The game then settled to a steady pattern, swift through balls to the two front-runners in the Celtic, Bobby Lennox and Steve Chalmers, the men who were to carry the attacking threat on their own because of the absence of the wingers.

Sadly, too, it became too physical an encounter. It smouldered with the threat of an unexploded bomb, occasionally flashed dangerously near detonation, and just stopped short of major trouble.

Celtic left-half Jim Brogan was booked for a foul in 14 minutes – just after he had been warned by referee Jim Callaghan – but he could look back at the end and consider himself unlucky to be the only player whose name was in the referee's book.

Celtic's two defenders Jim Craig and Billy McNeill congratulate John Fallon after the game.

Fallon bravely beats Ferguson to the ball in a goalmouth scramble.

Rangers inside-left Willie Johnston seemed to appoint himself the agitator of the Celtic defence. It was a dreadful mistake for a player who was the Ibrox side's main goal-scoring hope, and yet became far too involved in flare-ups to help his team.

Celtic's tactics had been to let Rangers play around in mid-field, and then snap down on the Ibrox attacks as they built up near the Parkhead penalty area.

It had worked well, apart from one shot from John Greig which cannoned off 'keeper John Fallon and away from the onrushing Ferguson.

Still, these are games where planning can be wrecked by one slip, one flaw in a move could have destroyed that Celtic lead.

Obviously they wanted another goal for half-time, just as certainly Rangers were desperate for an equaliser. I don't imagine either team could have visualised as the minutes ticked away to the interval what that score would eventually be.

For in two fantastic minutes the score-line swept from that narrow one goal difference to a yawning gap of three goals for Celtic.

It started apparently far away from the danger zone, just inside Rangers half on the main stand side.

A miss-directed pass went out to Rangers outside-left Orjan Persson, I suppose in most games he would have let it go out, these are matches where players try to get the ball at all costs.

As he tried to tame it and the ball bounced awkwardly young George Connelly stepped in, and slid the ball past Rangers left-back Willie Mathieson to Bobby Lennox.

Numbers mean nothing in modern football. Lennox, with the number 10 on his pants, was in the inside-right spot as he sped in on a direct line for goal.

As he stepped inside the penalty box, and Mathieson desperately tried to retrieve the situation, Lennox coolly looked up and drove the ball away past 'keeper Martin.

It must have been a magic moment for the little man, who had suffered a season of missed chances, the agony that hits all strikers at some time.

Like goalkeepers, theirs is the most vulnerable of positions. There is rarely a second chance, Lennox did not need one.

The frantic cheering of the Celtic end, the sullen silence of the Rangers end . . . there was hardly time for fans to sneak looks at watches to see how long until half-time before incredibly the ball was again in the back of the Rangers net.

It was an amazing blunder by the Ibrox defence. 'Keeper Martin had taken a short goal-kick, to John Greig. As the Ibrox skipper tried to turn with the ball he lost it to Connelly as the youngster for the second time in two moves by him, swooped on a slowness by Rangers.

And it was then that the 20 year old playing in his first Cup Final, showed the coolness and authority of a veteran.

Many players, and more experienced than Connelly, would have just tried to bang the ball into the net.

But he held on to the ball, smartly side-stepped 'keeper Martin and rolled the ball into the net.

'An old head on young shoulders' was his manager's quick verdict on him after the game.

Gift goals? Slips by Rangers players helped to make them, but the significant feature was they were forced into them by Celtic players, who then exploited them.

Celtic never looked like easing off that commanding lead in the second-half, the chance of another turn-up to somersault Rangers back into the game was not given to the Ibrox side.

A Lennox header bounced off the bar, and then in 77 minutes Chalmers scored the fourth with a dash down the left and as the Rangers defence, who had vainly appealed for offside, regrouped and waited for a pass to Lennox, the inside-right slammed the ball into the net between Martin and McKinnon.

Fallon clutches the ball from a corner.

The second-half too, had its share of nastiness. But in one moment Bobby Murdoch by keeping his temper, saved a situation which could have inflamed the terracing.

As he and Alex Ferguson walked up to take position for a corner the Ranger, for no apparent reason, seem to butt Murdoch.

The Celt shrugged it off . . . and in that one moment was a worthy winner of the 'Player of the Year' trophy.

Where did it go wrong for Rangers? I believe that they had come to rely too much on Colin Stein, and a team based on one man will always run into trouble.

Too many of their players seemed prepared to chuck it, and they struggled to find any semblance of form.

Where did it go right for Celtic? It showed once again the power of the Parkhead pool, and the fact that they could adapt to different tactics.

They had played all season with Johnstone and Hughes as the key-men of their attack, yet they slotted in perfectly into a plan which was the exact opposite, one without wingers.

It would not be a Cup Final without heroes. Celtic had two of them, George Connelly, drafted into the first team for his first full match since October and playing as if he had never been out.

And 'keeper John Fallon, who for so long looked as if his career was

Martin saves a high ball from McNeill.

going to be fatally affected by the disaster of the 1968 New Year game against Rangers.

I liked the way Jim Craig and Billy McNeill rushed to him at the end and presented the 'keeper to the crowd . . . a nice touch!

The road to Hampden had started in January with a shock result, a 3–3 draw against Partick Thistle at Firhill, after Celtic had lead 2–0, then 3–1.

It was a last-minute equaliser by inside-left Jimmy Bone which gave Thistle the second chance . . . they must have wondered after the replay if it had been worth it.

For in that game Celtic touched one of their high peaks of the season to crush Thistle by 8–1.

There was a disaster for them in the next round, when they went to Shawfield for a game that had been postponed because of the weather.

'Keeper Ronnie Simpson brilliantly dived at the feet of Clyde centre Jimmy Quinn, and was taken off with a dislocated shoulder.

Tommy Gemmell eventually took over in goal, and the game ended in a 0–0 draw, although Clyde failed to take any advantage of the emergency 'keeper.

Celtic won the replay 3–0, the week after their draw in Milan and met St. Johnstone in the quarter-final.

Again they let the opposition sneak back into the game and won

Lennox scores the Celts second goal.

eventually 3–2. And in the semi-final they had to fight off a quick goal by Morton, before they eventually won 4–1.

So they moved to that emphatic final victory, a result which on football merit no one could dispute.

But there were disturbing aspects from the game, not all connected with the football. Too often the match itself had threatened to spill over into violence transmitting itself from the field to the terracing.

Fortunately the only crowd break-in – after Celtic had scored their fourth goal – turned out to be thousands of Rangers fans trying to find a quicker way out of the ground.

But any break-in is one too many. There is still the chance of some drunken idiot running on to the park and assaulting a player.

It is becoming more obvious that a big crowd at 'Old Firm' games is nearly uncontrollable. It is almost impossible for police to effectively pick out all the trouble-makers in a packed terracing.

It took one fan twenty-five minutes to fight his way from near the foot of the terracing to the top because the passage-ways were choked.

Football has dodged for too long taking any real preventative action, programme appeals have been shown to be worthless.

Anyone who attends these matches knows that the question of solving the problem and bringing the supporters together seems as far away as ever.

I feel one solution would be to restrict the gate to an attendance of 40,000, and beam the match on closed-circuit TV to Ibrox, if Rangers are playing at Parkhead, or the Celtic ground if they are at Ibrox.

For the sake of football's image I hope we do not have to wait for the ultimate horror, death on the terracing, before some really effective action is taken.

Bobby Murdoch

If a careers prospectus was made up for kids planning a career in football what would the identikit picture of the modern soccer star look like?

I expect many of the fans who fill the stadiums every week or watch their idols flit across the TV screens would give an answer with a description resembling a refugee from the chorus of 'Hair'.

If your son has not got a moustache, long hair or sideburns don't put him into football would seem to be the message from the football fields of Britain.

It is the time in football when the world of pop and soccer have merged, when the screams of girl fans at an Ireland-England international when George Best touches the ball can rival any roars from the male section of the Belfast crowd.

Fortunately Best produces his own inimitable brand of football magic, as well as fulfilling his role in his girl fans eyes of star swinger of the sixties.

But sometimes the long-haired look can help a player get his picture in the papers, even when his ability is not so high.

So, if looking along a team group picture makes you itch to get your hands on a pair of barber's scissors, relax.

Football ability alone can still count, and as witness for the defence I call Bobby Murdoch.

He is the opposite of the image of today's stars. He is smartly dressed in well-tailored suits, he has a short styled hair-cut, with his solid bulk on the park he is almost a throw-back to a wing-half of the thirties.

Player of the year . . . Celtic's Bobby Murdoch with his trophy after the presentation by Scottish Football Writer's Association annual dinner in Glasgow.

And above all he can play football!

He took the Scottish Football Writers Association 'Player of the Year' trophy in 1969 with a runaway victory of more than half the votes, an unusually high percentage for any winner.

His manager, Jock Stein, rarely given to either public praise or condemnation about his own players, sometimes forgets himself in any discussion when Murdoch's name crops up.

'He is the best player in Britain,' he will say adding a look which defies any argument and with the authority of an accolade coming from Stein which most players would regard as equal to a call from Buckingham Palace.

And it may be that Murdoch, still only 24, is standing only on the edge of football greatness.

Now he is more assured, more ready to state his views on football, but always it is a professional outlook.

At the official banquet after the World Cup international against West Germany – when his last-gasp equaliser had given Scotland a face-saving draw – a foreign journalist said to him: 'Murdoch, you are one of the top ten stars in Europe.'

He smiled, thanked the journalist for his compliment and then had a lengthy discussion with him about the European football scene.

But later he said to me: 'You know, it's nice when somebody says that to you, but I don't see myself as one of the stars of Scotland, or for that matter Celtic.

'That's big Tam Gemmell, or wee Jimmy, or Yogi. I am a professional, I just want to get on with the game.'

Newspapermen have to listen to a lot of statements from people in football which you know are untrue even before they have finished the sentence.

But I believe Murdoch. And for someone whose views are not presented so very often in public he has some surprising and forthright opinions.

'People said after we won the three domestic trophies, what a pity you missed the European Cup.

'Well, so it was, the team were just as upset as the fans. But you know, I think it is impossible to have another clean sweep.

'Everything is compared with 1967 when we won every trophy, but I don't expect that will happen again in the same season.

'I think we will win every one of the trophies again – well, we've already done it with the domestic trophies – and I believe we will do it again with the European Cup, but not all together.

'The pressures become harder. The first year we were in the European Cup, we were the great unknowns.

'I don't mean that teams took it easy against us, but our style was still unknown to them.

'Now they know all about us. Look at wee Jimmy Johnstone, he's as famous on the continent as George Best.

'Teams put a pack of defenders round him. We are up with Real Madrid, Benfica and Manchester United. We are ex-holders, so everyone wants to knock us out.

'Of course, you balance that up with experience. You get used to playing with these pressures. A good team can overcome it, and I think we are a good team.'

Murdoch has forthright views on another controversial aspect of modern football . . . dirty play.

He is a player who as a teenager was robust, and in his early twenties it brought him two ordering-offs, although there was an element of bad luck about both of them.

The first was against St. Mirren in a league game at Parkhead. He claims still it was a remark made to a linesman by another Celtic player, but to his own and the club's credit they did not present it as a defence.

The second ordering-off was against Dynamo Kiev in the European Cup in Russia, when Celtic's short-lived reign ended with a first-round defeat.

An over-fussy Italian referee Antonio Sbardella sent him off after having already cautioned him for throwing away the ball at free-kicks.

It was the blackest moment of his senior career, and although his action was an irritation which football could do without few referees would have matched the severe action of the Italian for the offence.

'I listen sometimes to players, especially the Anglos at international get-togethers. The conversation is amazing. They are busy talking about players in the opposing teams their side had been detailed to kick out of a game.

'I don't believe that's football,' he says forcibly.

The influence of his manager comes through some of his talk. 'I believe we should still try to entertain the crowd. I don't believe in a game where there are no tackles, but I don't accept the theory that you have to half-kill opponents.'

It was one of Jock Stein's most significant moves when he rejoined Celtic to push Murdoch back from the inside-forward position, where he tended to toil a bit, to the right-half spot.

He had only played at wing-half a few times since his first-team debut as a 17 year old away back in August 1962.

Murdoch was another of the apparently endless stream of bright youngsters Celtic discovered, but could not blend into a winning formation.

And he had the added impact of having been discovered by no less a person than the club chairman, Bob Kelly, himself.

He served an apprenticeship with his team-mates which too often had a bitter taste about it. As they march up now to the rostrum at Hampden for their winners' medals I imagine they must still glance

A sight to make goalkeepers' tremble . . . as the ball blurs its way from the right foot of Bobby Murdoch at a Celtic training session.

down at the losers waiting below, a position where they themselves stood for so long.

Murdoch was in two finals beaten by Rangers, the League Cup and the Scottish Cup, but even at that time a rival on the Ibrox side, Jim Baxter, could mark him down as a player with special promise.

The trouble with most of the Celtic babes of his era was that they were given too spectacular a time-table to become a success.

When Bobby made his bow Pat Crerand, the man whose position he eventually took over, predicted . . . 'In six months he will be a wonder player, and a Scottish international.'

The forecast did come true, but everyone was so desperate for success that every new boy was hailed as the player who would lead them to the end of the honours famine.

It was after Stein moved him back that the true football style of Murdoch really flourished. His sweeping passes out of defence – he must be one of the most accurate movers of a ball in the game – are one of the great sights of football today.

But perhaps because goals are the end product of it all it is his scoring efforts which have won him most fame.

The tally is 91 goals, and I once heard an opponent say almost wistfully: 'He never scores a soft goal.'

They scream into goal. Full-blooded shots racing past the 'keeper to bullet the back of the net. Goals to be run over time and again in the play-back of one's memories.

I remember two against Wales in 1965, two against Dynamo Kiev in 1966, one against Hibs in the game after the Russian team had defeated Celtic two seasons later, one against Red Star last season, and the West German equaliser.

The one he picks out was the second goal of a 2–0 victory for Celtic against Rangers in a league game at Parkhead in 1966.

'I got the ball in the centre of the defence, saw a gap in the Ibrox line-up and managed to hit it over all their heads and 'keeper Billy Ritchie as he came out.'

I don't think Murdoch picked it because it was against Rangers – although the feeling of jubilation in either team when they score against the other has a special tang to it.

However he does not seem to share the same intense feeling which sometimes wraps itself around Celtic that every newspaperman is either an open or a secret Rangers fan.

What about the problem which sometimes perturbs the terracing and press juries . . . is he putting on too much weight?

Certainly he can look pretty bulky in his green-and-white hooped strip, but Murdoch himself denies he has a weight problem.

'I have not put on much weight, and I watch what I eat,' he says. Still, for someone who is so solidly built it's obviously a factor which will have to be guarded as he gets older.

Perhaps part of the apparent slowness last season came because he played for most of the season with the legacy of an ankle injury.

He damaged his ankle ligaments playing for the Scottish League against the League of Ireland in Dublin, and when he came back it sometimes meant disguising the injury during matches.

Murdoch typically dismisses it. 'I got over it.' But his manager told me after the season was over . . . 'It was only in the last month of the season that he was really one hundred per cent fit. It was a great effort by him.'

Stein believes that Murdoch would be an even better player if he played only once a week, something not possible in the tightly-crammed British fixture lists, because of his energy-sapping role in the very heart of the team.

His standard is so high that I heard one commentator say after the international against Wales at Wrexham . . . 'He'll need to watch, he's slowing up a bit.'

Yet it was obviously completely ignoring the fact that it was Murdoch's fourth game in a week, including the nervous tension of a Scottish Cup Final, and was the reason for fairly quiet games by him and his opposite number in the Rangers team, John Greig, who also had played four games, in the international side.

When Cesare Maldini, the assistant coach for A.C. Milan was praising Murdoch, the Celtic boss told him: 'Yes, and what a player in your match set-up of one game a week.'

Fortunately, despite a bid from Boca Juniors, the Argentine team, Murdoch, who is vice-captain of the club, is happy to stay in Scotland.

Celtic's success march can never be pinpointed to one player, but I imagine in a poll of opposition managers he is the one player in the Parkhead squad they would like to see sitting on the sidelines.

After Dunfermline had drawn 1–1 with Slovan Bratislava in the semi-final of the European Cup Winners' Cup their manager George Farm was conducting the after-the-match press conference.

There was a slightly dismal air about it, for everyone had hoped for a first-leg lead from the match.

One journalist remarked to Farm: 'You could have done with a Bobby Murdoch in the middle of the field.'

Farm looked at him, and then quelled him with the instant reply: 'Yes, and so could seventeen other clubs in the First Division.'

Defeat by Milan

Jock Stein stood in the middle of the crowded banqueting hall. He was flanked on one side by his chairman, Sir Robert Kelly, on the other by Milan president, Franco Carraro.

He clutched the giant sword of honour, encased in its black leather scabbard, with which he had just been presented (previous holders Sir Matt Busby, Sir Stanley Matthews and Pele) and said:

'I just wish I had been given this before the game. It would have helped me cut a way through the Milan defence.'

The audience of soccer V.I.P's and journalists from all over Europe laughed at Stein's wry comment . . . for only a few hours before his dream of a second European Cup win for Celtic had disappeared, the hopes now as cold as the bitter March weather.

It was the night of the 1–0 shock defeat for Celtic on their own Parkhead from A.C. Milan. The game that had sent Scotland's football temperature soaring with a severe case of European Cup fever had ended . . . and the inquests had begun.

After-the-match banquets are tilted according to the results. If the home side, as hosts, have won there is a jubilant atmosphere about the place. A defeat tends to have the lingering air of the last supper.

Three years previously I had watched Matt Busby, at a similar function in a Manchester hotel, affably welcome guests after a European Cup semi-final defeat against the almost unrated Partizan of Belgrade, yet privately he must have wondered if United's last chance of European success under his management had disappeared.

How do managers react on such occasions, when it must be hard to force a smile, harder still to talk to people whose views on the game may make you want to choke?

At the vital quarter-final stage of the European Cup it must be hard to win nothing but the accolade of a 'good loser', and deep down no real professional is that in any job.

It may seem to state the obvious, but defeat and Jock Stein are not familiar or happy partners. His reaction after some defeats has been bitter, yet that night, when I imagine he would have most liked to have gone home and shut his own front door he stood in that hotel room and faced the world.

As the guests sipped their drink, and munched their way through the buffet supper Stein placed himself in the middle of the floor.

He did not tuck himself away at a side table. He planted his massive bulk solidly in front of the buffet table, and talked to anyone who wanted to speak to him.

A word with German team boss Helmut Schoen, a long talk with the visiting Manchester United delegation headed by assistant manager Jimmy Murphy.

And a constant conveyor belt of Italian journalists, whose teams seem to take more people along with them to record their matches than any other country.

The insistant pleas . . . 'Signor Stein, I must talk with you for ten minutes,' one of which brought an answer . . . 'Do you get as long as that with Rocco?'

But eventually they were all satisfied, and among the last to leave – as the waiters cleared up the party debris – were Stein and his wife.

However, when the party was over, and in the harsh reality of the day after, no party spirit could hide the disappointment which rippled through Celtic, right from the chairman down to the ball boys.

The simple fact was in the 99-day span, from the draw which brought the Scottish league champions against the Italian league champions until the final whistle in Glasgow, Celtic had lived with this game.

It had always been around. Sometimes, with the pressure of the league championship and the Scottish Cup, it had been pushed temporarily into the background.

But eventually it became the all-consuming interest, for no European Cup-tie outside the final had ever captured the imagination of the public.

It was more than a defeat, it seemed as if a way of life had ended. It had not of course, if you looked at Celtic's future programme for the rest of the season a quick glance showed that they were still interested

Your choice, Mr. McNeill! Spanish referee Ortiz de Mendibil checks with Celtic skipper Billy McNeill before he spins the coin to decide ends in the European Cup match, as Milan skipper Gianni Rivera looks on.

in the three Scottish trophies.

But that was the cold, clinical angle. Football is not made up of that kind of approach, and Scotland wallowed in the worst of all soccer ailments, anti-climax, for at least a few days after the Milan result.

There is no doubt that a clash against the Italian teams can arouse more interest in Scotland than matches against any other country. Perhaps because, since the great Real Madrid team slipped slowly into retirement, the household names – the continental players whose fame knows no national boundaries, have belonged mainly to Italy.

It was a tie in which the public could hardly fail to be interested. They had it plugged at them remorselessly day by day for almost three months.

So let's look at the anatomy of a European Cup match, the men involved and their methods.

The Italians are masters of soccer gamesmanship and two days after the draw the first shots in the lengthy campaign were fired when Milan announced that former centre-half Cesare Maldini, one of the heroes of their 1963 Cup Win – and who had played against Celtic on the North American close-season tour the previous summer – would spy on the Scots side.

When Maldini did arrive the tall handsome Italian, who looked as if he had just wandered off a Rome film set, put into words a sentiment which thousands of fans, both in Scotland and Italy, believed.

'This is a game that should have been kept for the final,' he said. 'Now one of us must go out, it is bad for football that we cannot both be there when the final is played. But this will be a great, great game.'

And after that neat little bit of public relations he whizzed off with Jock Stein for a tour of possible hotels.

Maldini saw Celtic drop a point to relegation-threatened Falkirk . . . the first of three points they were to lose in successive matches as the weather gave a grim warning of the ice-bound pitches which were to cause such fixture chaos.

His summing-up was simple; he spotlighted Bobby Murdoch as the Celtic key-man, and he took a swipe at the conditions.

'I must say that in Italy we would not have been asked to play on such a ground. That was suitable for ice hockey, not football.'

The next week-end Jock Stein and his assistant Sean Fallon took their look at Milan, when they saw them win 1–0 against Torino in the giant San Siro Stadium.

It gave them a glimpse of something they already knew, the defensive quality of Italian soccer, and Milan's coach Nereo Rocco complained the game had been ruined by the opposition's obstructive tactics.

So the spy merry-go-round went on, consuming newspaper space in that spell around Christmas when it seems strangely silent before the New Year holiday programme rush.

Maldini came back to see Celtic lose by a John Greig penalty to Rangers at Ibrox in the New Year's league fixture.

And the next day the boss himself, Nereo Rocco, followed to take his own look at Celtic in a league match against Dunfermline at Parkhead.

Again, it was the Italians at their most diplomatic. Rocco forecast: 'Either Milan or Celtic will win the European Cup this season. It is the only possible solution to the competition. We are the two strongest teams left.'

Rocco did not seem too concerned about Celtic's Ibrox defeat. He dismissed it by saying: 'It is a game like our own clashes with Inter-Milan back home. A local derby, anything can happen.

'This trip is just a curiosity one for me. My helper Cesare Maldini has already looked at Celtic and their players. His opinions have always been right in the past.'

Then Rocco, with the shocked horror that all Continentals have when they look at British clubs' tightly packed fixtures said: 'My main interest is to see how much Celtic can react to such an exacting period of matches in such a short time . . . four matches in eight days seems impossible.

'In Italy this would not be allowed, it seems crazy to have such a system.'

He saw Celtic gain a 3–1 victory against Dunfermline, and buzzed back home just as soon as the final whistle had sounded, to neatly dodge the posse of waiting press-men who wanted to know what he thought of the 'impossible', after he had seen it.

That was the last of the spy jaunts, and next to take over in the spotlight was the problem of dates for the actual matches.

It's all an essential part of the preliminaries . . . the shadow boxing before the fight.

After long negotiations, with the clubs and the Scottish Football Association involved the problem was sent, as is almost inevitable, to the headquarters of the organisers, the European Football Union in Berne.

As fixed dates will soon be brought in for all the rounds we should be spared these somewhat boring formalities, and the European Union a few headaches.

However, on 8 January, more than a month after the draw, it was finally fixed, 19 February in Milan and 12 March in Glasgow, the dates Celtic wanted.

Yet with that question out of the way these astute Italians knew just how to continue their war of nerves. This time the approach was different, they were trying to convince Celtic of all the worries they had.

And at the beginning of February they announced that a psychiatrist would be called in because Milan were not scoring goals, their tally at the time was sixteen goals from sixteen championship matches.

Rocco, with all the solemnity of an eminent doctor giving a medical bulletin on a famous patient, said unhappily: 'The trouble is that they have lost their will-power. They don't fight for the ball the way they should, and of course, they do not get goals any longer.

89

'Because we have not scored regularly we have been strongly criticised. This has not helped the team, it has increased their depression.'

It brought the terse comment from Jock Stein . . . 'I will not be surprised at anything the Italians try.'

However, I must admit that despite the part he played in the pre-match war of nerves I liked Rocco.

Such quotes as – 'Stein played a centre-half, Ron Yeats, at centre-forward for Scotland against Italy in Naples. Even the Italians have never done that' – only shows that the Milan coach is as much a victim of the Italian system of outrageous statements as anyone else.

But the man who is the second highest taxed person in his home city of Trieste, and who speeds along the autostrada in his Alfa Romeo to supervise his twin interests of football in Milan and a ship's chandlers business in Trieste, is nobody's fool.

I met him last year on the tour of North America when his side drew with Celtic in New York and were defeated by them in Toronto.

We were chatting at an informal moment at a press conference in the plush Royal York Hotel in Toronto (proudly billed as the largest in the British Commonwealth).

It was the day after Manchester United's win against Benfica in the European Cup Final at Wembley.

The club's official press relations officer interpreted with a mixture of some Italian, some English phrases as we talked, a little oasis of soccer chat in a country not really too concerned about football.

Rocco looks like an Italian Jock Stein. He has the same open face, the same crinkly hair-style, and although he is not as tall as the Celtic boss his bulk gives him an appearance of height.

He shrugged his shoulders, waved his hand to punch home his point and said: 'Britain will keep the European Cup for the next two seasons.

'We all expected the British would break through some time in the European Cup. Now they are the bosses they will be difficult to beat, perhaps it will take another two years.'

I wonder if the thought ever flashed through his mind again before the two games!

Certainly he snapped his way through the final preliminaries. Celtic, caught in the prolonged bad weather, had a free Saturday before the first game when their match with Morton was postponed.

But the Italians only managed to struggle to a 1–0 win away from home at Pisa, with the present of an own goal from the opposition.

Jock Stein had laid on the line the tactics his players were going to use. At their Troon training headquarters, which Milan were to use when they came to Scotland, he said:

'We are going to reveal the other European face of Celtic in Italy. I love attacking football, that's the way we played in Lisbon, and all Europe loved it that night.

'But Lisbon was ninety minutes of death or glory. When the final whistle blows in Milan the game will only be half over.

'The sad fact is that as long as European Cup ties are two-legged a team must be two-faced.

'My plan is to play sensible soccer. We will be careful, not as cautious as we have been in some Continental matches, but we must get control in mid-field.'

So Stein and his squad set off from frozen Britain to frozen Italy, and the first of a lengthy series of press conferences as soon as we landed in Milan.

For the non-football addict who thinks that the Scottish press devotes too much space to soccer I can only say . . . consider yourself lucky you don't live in Italy.

Every detail is lovingly and minutely described. The exact time the Celtic players stepped off their chartered jet was recorded, every quote is not just noted by the reporters but also printed.

The moment when it all ended and a dream died . . . the dream of a second European Cup triumph. That awful moment as Milan's Prati shoots past 'keeper Fallon, and the Celtic defenders chasing him can do nothing about it, as he scores the winner.

The Celtic training headquarters were at Varese, an hour's coach drive out of Milan, and in an hotel perched at the top of a mile's climb from the town.

It was a breathtaking tourist scene, like a part of the film set of 'Dr. Zhivago'. The heavy snow muffled any other sounds, the hotel sat there wrapped in a blanket of total silence.

And after the Celtic players had scampered about the snow for their first loosening-up session just after they arrived that Monday afternoon the giant thermometer on the wall outside their hotel had dropped ominously to freezing point.

The players followed the usual routine of a training session on Tuesday, and then were taken into Milan for time off to do some shopping, and take a look at the stadium.

Stein had already hotted up the war of nerves before the match when he told Italian journalists he might not play Jimmy Johnstone because of the state of the pitch.

However, he was merely stringing Rocco along, although to the Italians the news was as sensational as the Brazilians leaving out Pele.

But the real pre-match story began while the Celtic players were in Milan.

Snow, which had threatened to come all day, finally began to fall, and went on and on, and on.

It was so bad that the Celtic team coach bringing them back from Milan could not complete its journey up the steep, winding private road to the hotel and the players had to walk it.

It was still snowing the next morning, and in the afternoon as the party relaxed, looking at a match on TV between Torino and Slovan Bratislava, later to meet Dunfermline in the European Cup-Winners' Cup.

It was still snowing as the team bus and the press coach started off for Milan, with chains on the tyres to assist in the first part of the journey.

And it was still snowing when we arrived at the San Siro Stadium to find a small army of ground-staff carefully sweeping the snow off the plastic and wood chips covering which protected the pitch from the worst of the weather.

Twice before the match they cleared the centre circle, twice it was obscured again by the swirling snow.

The Italian crowd, the most fanatical supporters in Europe, sent huge chunks of snow crashing down from one tier on to the helpless fans below them, some of whom had paid as much as £5 for their seat.

It was the most incredible, bizarre scene I have witnessed at any

European Cup match.

Rockets streamed down from the packed terraces on to the field, the whistles blew, the crowd bayed as they must have almost 2,000 years ago in Rome.

It was the nearest I have ever seen in crowd reaction to that dreadful afternoon in Buenos Aires when Celtic and Racing Club clashed in the second leg of the world championship.

We tend today to take European Cup matches almost too much for granted. They are as much a part of the soccer scene as any ordinary league fixture, jet travel has telescoped the travelling time between countries to almost insignificance.

Yet there are times when the differences between British and Continental atmosphere at matches are so marked that you would need to be a pretty cold-eyed observer not to be excited by it all.

It was to the Celtic players credit in that match that they did not let it affect them. In fact, it had the opposite effect.

Jimmy Johnstone told me: 'I felt it made me want to play good football just to show them.'

They started somewhat nervously, saw a goal for Milan correctly ruled offside, and then crept into the match themselves by half-time.

The conditions were atrocious. I am sure it was only because 72,000 fans were already in the stadium and German referee Kurt Tschenscher had started the match that he allowed it to carry on.

A thin mist hung over the far side of the pitch, a white ball was used which was almost impossible to pick out on the snow-covered pitch.

Celtic chairman Sir Robert Kelly afterwards claimed that the match should not have been played because the lines were obliterated, and certainly they could not be seen from the press-box.

But apparently nearer the ground, and as far as the players were concerned, they could be seen which no doubt influenced the referee to carry on the match.

Celtic had a second-half scare when a header from centre-forward Sormani glanced off a post.

But it was the Scots – breaking the tactics of not attacking away – who provided one of the game's most memorable moments with one dazzling solo run by left-winger John Hughes which left a trail of floundering defenders and ended with 'keeper Cudicini springing to a superb save.

Jim Brogan was injured in the second-half in a clash with Milan skipper Gianni Rivera and Bertie Auld was substituted, but with a little care Celtic could have taken a lead from that first leg.

However, as the final whistle went and the last rockets showered down from the terrace, and a few bonfires sputtered out, the triumph was Celtic's.

To look back now, free from the frustration of the Glasgow game, it was a marvellous result in Milan. No Scottish team had ever even managed to draw against either A.C. Milan or Inter-Milan in the San Siro Stadium.

Yet there is always an odd feeling at these games for the journalists, a little pocket of Scotland, in a sea of foreign faces.

It sometimes seems hard to believe it has been a good result. There are no cheers for such a score.

You make your way to the dressing-room pushing past a trail of departing Italians, whose gloom wraps itself round the stadium.

And then finally we were in the only place in that whole giant stadium where there was an avalanche of noise.

Jock Stein stood in one corner, in a grey cardigan, looking as if he had enjoyed a relaxed evening in front of his TV set.

Little Jimmy Johnstone, a green towel wrapped around his waist, chattered to a mob of clamouring Continental journalists, and radio microphones were stuck in front of his face.

A German journalist, used to the strict discipline of Continental teams, murmured to me in amazement: 'Look at them. They are the most feared team in Europe yet they are as happy as schoolboys.'

Yet, in the midst of happy players, and shouting pressmen, Stein was to make a remark which seemed only diplomatic at the time but was to take on an awful significance.

'It was a magnificent result and I am delighted. It was just what we wanted, however, we have still to win in Glasgow and the tie is not yet over against a team of this class.'

The contrast in the adjoining dressing-room was greater than it had ever been on the field. The coldest spot in that freezing concrete canyon was the A.C. Milan home dressing-room.

Strong-arm security men guarded it for 45 minutes before it was opened for Rocco to give a short, sharp press conference.

He and Stein wrapped their arms around each other, and then everyone trooped back out into the snow.

The scene now moved to Scotland, and something which I would not have thought possible, there was more fan pre-match reaction than in Italy. Glasgow went European Cup crazy.

A bookmaker paid £30 for two 50/- stand tickets, a businessman advertised for tickets and was offered three at £120.

The people who possessed these precious 75,000 bits of cardboard

The bitter, bitter taste of defeat. The final whistle has gone, Celtic are out of the European Cup and these expressions tell the whole story as Bobby Murdoch and Billy McNeill glumly wait for the Italians to leave the field.

The wonderful feeling of victory. . . . Milan coach Nereo Rocco rushes on to the Parkhead pitch to hug his delighted players after their European Cup win.

were the kings of Glasgow, something to be waved in front of their workmates as a token of triumph.

Both teams were hit by pre-match injuries. Milan did not bring centre-forward Sormani and wing-half Trappatoni, and they had doubts about forward Piero Prati.

Celtic had one casualty, Bobby Lennox, injured against Raith Rovers the previous Saturday, and not even walks in the chilling sea at the training camp could get him fit to play.

But Prati did play, with devastating consequences on the whole Celtic European Cup campaign.

The game started smoothly for Celtic, following their manager's instructions to play the waiting game.

He reckoned that even if they did not get a quick goal, they need not panic. Time would be on their side.

But, as Stein himself has so often repeated, matches are not won by coaches but by players. And Celtic were to enjoy the luxury of time on their side for only twelve minutes.

Then came the disaster. Just inside his own half right-back Jim Craig took a throw-in to centre-half Billy McNeill.

It was a simple business of collecting the ball and sending it downfield, something McNeill must have done a thousand times in his career.

Tragically for him, this was the time he didn't. As he dithered with the ball, it slid away from him as Prati, at centre-forward, darted in and whipped towards goal.

The Celtic defence were caught wide out, they could do nothing as Prati charged on, and like a soccer horror film spinning on for them it ended only when the Italian shot the ball past 'keeper John Fallon.

A second before he scored I glanced down from the press-box to where McNeill, helplessly stranded in the middle of his own half, had suddenly realised Prati was going to score and buried his head in his hands.

And I thought back to something Jock Stein had written in his newspaper column before the first Milan game . . .

'Always there is the unexpected factor. That's what football is all about, and the team who can overcome it will win.'

Celtic were never really to recover from the blow. They should have had a penalty just after half-time when Malatrasi handled inside the box, but the Spanish referee turned down the appeal.

Time which had been their friend became their enemy. The game was completely transformed, tailor-made to the tactics the Italians perfect week-by-week in their own league . . . grab a goal and hang on to it.

Celtic worked, but I thought they never really got one clear chance to score. Half-chances certainly – maybe on another not so tense occasion they would have taken them – but nothing from which a player had the time to stop and steady himself.

Substitutions were made, Bertie Auld for Jim Brogan, Santin and Rognoni for Schnellinger and Hamrin.

But the star of the night was Milan's captain Gianni Rivera – the golden boy inside-forward, the man the Italians call the 'Bambino d'Oro.'

Tommy Docherty watching the game, said: 'He is like a ghost. You can't pin him down.'

Rivera masterminded their moves, but admitted later: 'This was the hardest game we have ever played, and certainly it is the best victory we have had.'

Rocco hurled his arms around Jock Stein in the Milan dressing-room and said: 'We have done the impossible.'

An Italian journalist told me later that Rocco had privately conceded to the club's top officials before the game that they would lose 4–0.

So it was all over, the dream of a second European Cup triumph, and most important of all, the chances of a clash with Manchester United which had been snatched away.

The hope of a meeting between the two British teams who had won the European Cup had aroused the whiff of combat in the Scots, always anxious to take on any team from England.

Celtic at least went out with dignity. Waved back by their manager, they stood and applauded the Italians off the field.

It was a small action, but one which was seen all over Europe on TV and brought them many messages complimenting on it. The team who had been vilified the season before, had shown that they could be beaten and take it.

Instead of European medals there were only the transistor radios shaped like a book, which Milan presented to the players and press.

But, of course, for the team there was the bitter, numbing, gnawing feeling of emptiness, which only a defeat in a major competition can bring.

The terracing feelings were summed up by a fan with a green and white scarf wrapped round his neck as we jostled away from the stadium.

'I'll never go into an Italian fish and chip shop again,' he vowed.

But he would, for like Celtic, he would finally get over it.

Stein . . . the Man and his Methods

The best unsolicited tribute to Jock Stein came from the chairman of an opposition First Division side, whose team had just been swept aside by the soccer whirlwind called Celtic.

The club chairman took him aside in the board-room and as Stein sipped his customary Coke joked: 'We were all jogging along making a living until you arrived.'

But it was a joke with the ring of truth, for it was a revolution which Stein and his methods brought to Scottish football, and one which fortunately many clubs have tried to follow.

That revolution gave the most important people in football – the fans – a real glimpse of another soccer world which most of them had seen on their television screens and seemed to be the copyright of European teams such as Real Madrid and Benfica.

Of course, no one, least of all Stein himself, would claim that there was no good football played by Scottish teams in Europe before his Celtic side.

The Baxter-inspired Rangers European Cup side of 1964–5 might have won it, but it all ended in the dying moments of the Prater Stadium on a freezing December day as Baxter fell to the ground with a broken leg.

It was a cruel finish to perhaps the most memorable of the Ibrox side's Continental displays, when they beat Rapide Vienna.

Bob Shankly's Dundee side, finally beaten at their first attempt in the European Cup in the semi-final against A. C. Milan, could perhaps have gone on to greater glory if they had been kept together.

The moments that make it all worth while! A jubilant Jock Stein races on to Parkhead to congratulate his team after the European Cup triumph against St. Etienne.

But it was the Celtic team of 1967 which did win it, something which only a few years earlier most fans would have considered as remote as landing a treble chance jackpot.

Scottish football until then could boast some of the biggest crowds in European matches, their fervour was matched by few nations, the press coverage the most intense.

However these were only fringe side-shows. It was winning the Cup, and becoming the first British team to succeed, which firmly put Celtic on the soccer map as one of the European elite.

Still, five ties in one season, even if they do land Europe's top club honour, are not the only part of Stein's success.

His greatest achievement is in making a success of a club where, before he arrived as manager, there was more talk of past glories and future promises than present achievement.

In the long grind of domestic soccer his Celtic side have managed to lift much of the drudgery out of the routine league programme by producing exciting football.

The box-office figures prove it. Any club needs to attract the floating football fan to boost their attendance, the type of fan who owes no allegiance to any team but picks his match Saturday by Saturday for the quality of the soccer.

Celtic's average attendance has jumped from 28,000 to 46,500 since he went to Parkhead.

His players call him 'The Big Man', this 46-year-old miner with a limp who, when he walks through the streets of football-mad Glasgow, makes more heads turn than Royalty.

What has spun Stein from a start in football 28 years ago as a £2-a-week player with unglamorous Albion Rovers to a position where he now drives, at speed, an expensive Mercedes and measures his salary with top business executives.

For a start, and it is an important start, he has a total commitment to football. He talks kindly about 'football people' as if they were a chosen race apart.

That list of 'football people' would include very few of the legislators who roll up to Hampden in the chauffeur-driven limousines as part of the official party on Cup final and international matches.

It would include some of his fellow-managers, trainers, players, referees and folk associated with football in a very humble way, but as long as they are dedicated to the sport they rate high in Stein's book.

He works fantastically long hours at his football, to the total exclusion of any hobbies except an occasional game of golf, and

This is how it's going to be done . . . and the Celtic first-team crowd around to listen to their manager at a tactics talk.

sometimes seems sceptical of other people in football who do not devote all their time to it.

But his secret is not just time spent working at, or watching, football. Plenty of other managers work just as hard, for not a tenth of the success his team has won.

Perhaps the answers lie behind the public face of Jock Stein in the part, which despite the fact that he is a manager, the fans never see.

The average fan on the terracing might spot him ducking into a dug-out, sometimes see a gloved hand shooting out waving instructions, or if he is on the pitch at a bad injury . . . but that is the only public glimpse they get during a game.

The real football face of Jock Stein is, as with any good manager, a complex mixture of regimental sergeant-major and sporting psychiatrist.

He overlords most of the Celtic training sessions himself, the sweat-lashed hours when the fitness which has helped to overwhelm so many opponents, is perfected.

An unknowing onlooker might find it a little odd, the sight of a middle-aged man looking a bit like a huge teddy-bear in a green track suit.

It's not odd to his players. I remember once watching a training session at the Hindu Country Club in Buenos Aires, the team's headquarters in that ill-fated World Championship attempt.

The manager was involved in one of his favourite training tactics, firing in shots at Ronnie Simpson.

The sweat poured off Simpson as he jumped and dived under the brassy Argentinian sun. He muttered to himself, but still the balls kept coming at him.

Yet that little episode, repeated at every training session, is one of the reasons why Ronnie's career stretched out well beyond a normal player's spell.

However, even as the shots sped at Simpson, there was still time for the manager, as if by some built-in X-ray, to whip round and tick off some member of another training group whom he considered as a bit slack with his work.

Away from the training ground at team tactics talks he can dissect an opposing team with the skill of a soccer surgeon, neatly spotting a weakness with instructions where his own team can pounce.

Part of this comes from an amazing total recall of moves during a game. Even when watching a TV re-run of a match he can tell at least ten moves before anyone else when an incident is coming up.

But perhaps the secret of the psychiatrist part was best summed up by Manchester United's Pat Crerand, a youthful wing-half under him when he was first at Parkhead as chief coach . . . 'Jock never asks a player to do something which is beyond him.'

Maybe that all sounds like a formula which should achieve the impossible, and win every game of football.

But Stein maintains firmly: 'There is always the unexpected in football. That's what makes it the game it is.

'The team who can overcome best the unexpected happenings during a game will be the winners.

'Anyway, players are not puppets. You don't sit in a dug-out and pull strings to make them jump.'

Although the spotlight has fallen on him in an era of a public and press very concerned with managers, it is when he talks about his

The man who once bossed Scotland, Jock Stein, and the man who is the present skipper, Billy Bremner, get together for a chat before a pre-season friendly . . . and Billy had the last laugh, Leeds won 2–1.

own players that he can become really excited.

Jock Stein may draw up the plans, but he has no misguided ideas about who carries them out.

I have heard him make scathing comments about referees, about the press, about legislators. But, at least to anyone outside the dressing-room, criticism of individual players, apart from disciplinary cases, is not made.

If there is to be criticism of the team's performance when they have had a bad game then it is kept in general terms, individuals are not named for a public witch-hunt.

Stein's face, Stein's quotes with a regular newspaper column and Stein's TV appearances – a more polished delivery now but still the same homely Lanarkshire accent – have made him one of the best-known men in Scotland.

Tommy Docherty once quipped: 'When my mother sends me the papers from Scotland, Jock's on the front page and Harold Wilson's on the back.'

He has made sure since he went back to Parkhead that Celtic's name is rarely out of the headlines. But the Sir Matt Busby diplomatic method of dealing with the press is not for him.

Stein tells a pressman if he does not like what has been written about his team. And few have not had the daunting task of facing up to a full-scale verbal explosion with him at some time.

It can be a shattering experience, but except in a very few cases, once the argument is over it is forgotten.

And, it is balanced by the fact that, especially abroad, few managers have a shrewder idea of when to release stories to give the maximum help to columnists struggling with communication difficulties.

Stein's public relations also include many visits to supporters' clubs, events which can have little interest for the national press but are important to his club's image just the same.

I think he would place alongside the team's success the fans' success in equal importance.

Bad behaviour by supporters – and although it has been good in Scotland a section of the Celtic fans have been notoriously trouble-prone on trips to England – concerns him deeply.

However, big crowds excite him. The day after the team returned from Lisbon speculation swirled round his future at Parkhead.

Ground-staff were still tidying up from the terracing the bits of litter left by the huge crowd who had packed the stadium the night before to welcome the team home.

The back-room boys! They are all former Celtic stars, many of whom do their work for the club out of the public eye, but with one aim . . . to keep the club at the top.

The line-up is (*left to right*): Jimmy McGrory (public relations officer), Neil Mochan (trainer), Sean Fallon (assistant manager), Willie Fernie (coach), John Higgins (chief Scout), John Duffy (scout), John McAlindon (groundsman), Alex Boden (coach), Jim Kennedy (supporters liaison officer), Frank Meechan (scout), Jock Stein (manager).

As the gold European Cup gleamed on the desk in his office, he told me: 'I love to see these crowds at a game, and I like to think my team has at least given them value for their money.

'That's one of the reasons I would find it very difficult to leave here.

'I used to find it heartbreaking at Dunfermline when sometimes there were only a few thousand in the ground for a game.

'Yet I believed then that I had a team as good as Celtic or Rangers but like so much of Scottish football, if only they had got a few more people in to watch how much better it would have been.'

The technical jargon which so many coaches sprinkle freely through their conversations is not used by Stein.

His concern is that the fans should be entertained, yet strangely enough, in his Dunfermline days – his first spell as manager – his reputation was more as a defensive-minded boss than one who favoured attack.

'I've listened to managers after a 0–0 draw tell you it was a great game. Maybe it was for them, with things happening right technically and tactically,' he says.

'But, with a few exceptions, if there are no goals, then it's not happening right for the fans.'

The Stein career has been written about a dozen times, it has been put in strip cartoon, it has become part of soccer legend.

How he left Albion Rovers for the obscurity of Welsh non-league side Llanelly . . . how he was rediscovered there by Celtic and brought back to coach their youngsters.

How he got a first-team chance and then captained the side to Coronation Cup triumph, and a League and Cup double.

How an ankle injury stopped him playing football, how he became chief coach with Celtic, then remade Dunfermline, revitalised Hibs, and returned to his greatest days at Parkhead.

Still, maybe in the myth that has been wrapped round a story that sounds as if it was a film screen-play, it's sometimes forgotten that all during these years the experience which finally flowered at Parkhead was being slowly built up.

Part of his success may also be that he does not wallow in nostalgia. He is grateful to players who have been in teams which won trophies for him, but he would just as soon talk about the promising kids on the Parkhead staff, than past achievements.

But sometimes there are occasional looks back into the past. He always claimed that watching the Hungarians conquer England at Wembley in 1953 – the first foreign team ever to achieve that – changed his football outlook.

And in his home he keeps a film of that game, with those 'Magical Magyars' led by Puskas, ripping England apart.

Stein has said he is unlikely to stay on as a manager after he is 55, that's in 1978. When you look at the pressures which have fallen on managers since 1958 there's no doubt they can only increase in the next ten years.

But, until then – and he is in a small elite band of managers in the happy position of saying when they will quit – it's likely that the world of soccer will still be sitting back in wonderment asking . . . 'What's that big man up to now?'

Celts in America

The modern soccer star's passport might make even James Bond envious. For on the buff-coloured pages are stamped the visas and entry signs of nations right round the world.

These are the gateway to a look at the world which the average fan could only dream about from peeps at exotic brochures, and which would cost even wealthy tourists a fair slice of their fortunes.

A hop across the Atlantic on a giant jet is now a common summer jaunt for Britain's top clubs, players can pick their way through the buzz and confusion of New York's Kennedy Airport as easily as Glasgow's Abbotsinch or London's Heathrow.

Twice in three years Celtic have made the trip to America and Canada. Their stars have wandered down Broadway, gazed at Niagara Falls, crossed the Golden Gate Bridge in San Francisco, and found out for themselves about Mexico City's much publicised altitude problem.

I suppose that the supporter back home reading stories of teams travelling to such spots as Miami, New York, Toronto, Mexico City, can only murmur with envy: 'What a life . . . and just to play football.'

Well, it is a wonderful life. But behind the glamour and excitement of these tours – and even the most experienced traveller can still get a thrill seeing again that wonderful New York sky-line – there is a double purpose.

These tours are usually a reward for a team's work during the season, and that 1968 tour celebrated the neat double of three successive League championships and League Cups.

Properly used the games can be a basis for plans a manager may have, but hesitates to try in the fierce combat of a normal season's programme.

Sometimes it can even be useful to try a player out of his position. I don't know if every full-back fancies himself as a centre-forward, but I remember a try-out Tommy Gemmell had at centre in a match in Bermuda, on a pitch which had a cricket wicket down the centre.

It was almost a cricket score, too! Celtic won 10–1 and Tommy scored two goals. But the experiment has not been repeated. Despite that score-line he really is more effective getting the goals as a full-back and not a fully fledged forward.

However, I know from that trip in 1966 that the basis for the European Cup triumph, crowned by the victory against Inter-Milan in Lisbon, was laid on the strenuous, eleven-match, five-week tour of America, Canada and Bermuda.

The 1968 tour was designed a little differently. The players were given almost a week off in the luxury of Miami, one of America's most famous holiday spots.

There were only three games, but all of them vital prestige matches. Two against the Italian champions, A.C. Milan – in New York and Toronto – and a top Mexican side, Nexaca.

Even in the midst of Miami's many tourist attractions, skin-diving, shark-fishing, golfing with go-carts to save walking between holes, there was football work to be done.

At one of the training sessions there was an injury to left-winger John Hughes, and another to Tommy Gemmell which kept both out of the first fixture against Milan, and eventually Gemmell flew home from Toronto for treatment.

The urgency to keep the team fit became even more important when A.C. Milan added the European Cup-Winners Cup to their honours with a victory against Hamburg in the final in Rotterdam.

Obviously twin victories against Celtic would boost their prestige, especially in their home city, where their close-neighbours, Inter-Milan, had failed a year before.

Matches with Italians can be dodgy in America. There is, of course, a strong Italian community who flock to get a nostalgic glimpse of their heroes of home.

Celtic were going back to play in the grandly named, but some-what ramshackle Roosevelt Stadium in Jersey City, New Jersey, across the Hudson River from New York.

Two years before in the sort of downpour which I thought was only conceived on a Hollywood movie set, they had held another Italian Club, Bologna, to a 0–0 draw, in the same stadium.

Flight delays mean time for a meal, but this trio (*left to right*) John Fallon, Ronnie Simpson and Steve Chalmers don't look too happy about it!

It had ended in a fans' riot as the supporters of the Italian side, incensed at their team's failure to win, sent a hail of bottles and missiles on to the pitch.

And my lasting memory is of an all-American cop, baton drawn, gun strapped to his side, charging up the aisles of the stand after the offenders . . . on a horse!

So it was perhaps understandable that two years later – even in the middle of the giddy New York sight-seeing round, including a visit to Madison Square Garden to see the World light-heavyweight fight between Dick Tiger and Bob Foster – Stein took time to tell his players . . . 'Keep cool, whatever happens.'

They needed to keep their heads cool! They did have to face another crowd problem, this time of too many people trying to get into the ground at the one time.

It was a scorching Sunday, but even these conditions can be turned

They're off . . . for the third trip across the Atlantic in two years. The glamour destinations, Miami, New York, Toronto, Mexico City. Who wouldn't be smiling with a schedule like that?

to advantage. It is a chance for a manager to see which players can overcome the conditions, for who knows when similar problems may come along in the European Cup.

However there was to be no quick appearance in the sun for the teams. They had to stay in their dressing rooms for 45 minutes, until the crowd trouble had cleared.

Yet it was anything but boring for the fans already in the ground, and those of us perched in the press-box above the stand . . . we got a side-show of our own.

The police control at the beginning was a bit slack. So hundreds of fans strolled on to the park, walked round the track, or simply sat down on the pitch.

Rival groups of supporters, waving their club banners, hurled chants at each other and turned the whole scene into an organiser's nightmare.

Over the loudspeaker came the repeated pleadings of an anguished Italian-American voice . . . 'Leave da field, pliz, leava da field.'

He could have saved himself the effort and enjoyed a cool beer in the sunshine. The trouble outside had been because there was not enough turnstiles open, and those that were had run out of change.

Eventually to get the 23,000 crowd into the ground, clear them off the field and get the game started it took the combined efforts of twenty squad cars of police and the help of mounted police.

There was no real ugliness. Just a crowd who added a preliminary to the main show, and had a ball to themselves at the same time.

The Celtic team which was fielded that day was . . . Simpson; Cattenach, O'Neil; Clark, McNeill, Brogan; Chalmers, Murdoch, Wallace, Gallagher, Lennox . . . with second-half substitutes McBride for Gallagher and Quinn for Chalmers.

Milan were without some of their stars, including their ace forward Rivera, who were with the Italian team in the European Nations Cup.

But Celtic lacked Jimmy Johnstone. The right-winger had been allowed to stay at home because of the strenuous season he had been through, and his famous dislike for flying.

Still, I think the Italians half-expected to see Jock Stein usher the little red-head on to the park. It was only after two games without him they were really convinced he had stayed at home.

The match was watched by Dunfermline, who were also on a North American tour and stayed in the same New York hotel as Celtic.

What a shrinking soccer world. Only two weeks before the teams had met in Scotland's last league game of the season, a clash between the Cup-winners and league champions at Dunfermline.

Willie Wallace put Celtic ahead in eleven minutes, but Milan equalised before half-time, and that's the way the score stayed until the end. It was a good result, considering that the Scots had not played a competitive match for a fortnight, and the pitch is really laid out more for baseball than soccer.

Part of the schedule for these tours is a constant round of banquets, civic lunches, official receptions.

Even in America there are supporters' club functions. After the Milan game Celtic were entertained by the Kearney branch. It's the second time I've been there . . . and if there is a more enthusiastic fan club I would like to meet them.

Some of their members fly over for many of the big games in Scotland, they listen to the results on a Saturday on a short-wave

The man who came home alone, Tommy Gemmell, who had to return
from the tour because of an injury, is met by his pretty wife, Anne, at
Prestwick Airport.

radio, and some even make the journey to New York every Sunday to keep right up to date with the British Sunday papers.

They made the long, tiring bus 'trip from New York to Toronto to support their side in the second game against Milan.

Like everyone else I reckoned they thought it was well worth while. That game, in the trim Canadian National Exhibition Stadium, was an epic.

It had a record crowd for a match in Canada of 30,121, a huge trophy and a 2,000 dollar prize to the winners . . . and a perfect result for Celtic.

It was also one of the few tour games I have watched in America and Canada which had the real atmosphere of a football match, not just the trimmings of a friendly game.

Maybe it was the stadium, situated only a couple of free-kicks away from the shores of Lake Ontario, and with a pitch suited for soccer, and not American football or baseball.

Maybe it was the crowd, fervent and knowledgeable – drawn from the sizeable Scottish and Italian communities of Toronto (sometimes a little too fervent, there were a few arrests).

Maybe it was the cold, grey drizzle to make the scene resemble home so much. But it all combined for a memorable match.

I remember the Italian coach, Nereo Rocco, with a red cap perched on top of his giant frame, leaping off his track-side bench to scream advice to his side.

But it was all in vain. This was a display of attacking football which has built Celtic their modern reputation.

Swift and incisive, they had been instructed to keep their crosses low and away from 'keeper Belli, who had gobbled up many of the cross-balls the previous Sunday.

Two minutes of the second-half had ticked away when Wallace put over a cross hardly head-high, the 'keeper blundered and Lennox blasted the ball home.

Then in sixty-four minutes came one of those great defence-splitting runs of John Hughes, which ended with Charlie Gallagher slamming home a second.

Celtic had another victory, another trophy, and the players a bit more spending money. And if the organisers had only hired an astrologist who could have predicted that the two teams would meet again in the European Cup, they could have really gone to town with the publicity they love so much over there.

It was a good victory especially as a reward for the Scottish exiles, who warmly descend on all visiting teams with loads of invitations.

Welcome home . . . for Billy McNeill, from wife Liz, daughter Susan and the twins, Libby and Carol.

Welcome home . . . for John Hughes, from his wife Mary and sons, Kevin and Martin.

Somehow, wherever you go there always seems to be more Scots turn up than English.

I remember one Spurs official on the 1966 tour when the London club had the same schedule for part of the trip, asking: 'How do you Scots get all the bleedin' invitations?'

But if the Canadian result was the most satisfying, the Mexican part of the tour was the most useful from the experimental point of view.

No modern Scottish side had played there, but twice Mexico would be the sports centre of the world, for the 1968 Olympic Games and the 1970 World Cup.

How would the altitude problem affect them? I think some of the players imagined we might have to strap on oxygen cylinders as soon as we landed after the long flight from Toronto.

Welcome home . . . for Bobby Murdoch, from his son Robert junior.

Instead there were guitar-strumming musicians to welcome us, and a bus which almost burst at the seams as players, officials, press and all the luggage was piled in. . . .

It's not always jet-style luxury on these tours. . . .

Celtic, like most teams away from home in another country, always try to train at the time of the kick-off of the actual match, and Mexico was no exception.

The players went through a rigorous training session, with stops for medical tests from the team doctor. Nobody seemed to be any the worse for it, but there was one flaw.

They had trained in a good, old-fashioned rain-storm (apart from Miami, that rain seemed to follow the tour), and perhaps the altitude effect had been minimised.

For the next night in the most impressive soccer stadium I have ever seen, the giant 105,000 seater Aztec Stadium, they learned all about it.

It had been a sultry day, turning the giant stadium into a concrete pressure-cooker, where the heat seemed to lie like a lid over the pitch.

Bang, Bang, Bang! Celtic were quickly three goals down, and nobody could remember when that had last happened. But worst of all, the team seemed listless, unable to mount their usual dashing raids or get back to help out in defence.

Right on half-time one of these so valuable goals of Billy McNeil gave them a lifebelt. And in the dressing-room at the interval they gratefully gulped down oxygen to aid them in the second-half.

Wallace pulled another back in the second-half, but the score stayed at 3–2 for Nexaca until the end. It was Celtic's first tour defeat in over three years.

However it had been a vital lesson. It showed that European teams would probably have trouble in the World Cup, but they could be overcome.

Every player had complained of some feeling of breathlessness, especially if they tried two fairly long runs in succession.

That Mexican match meant that Celtic were, as so often in recent seasons, the Scottish pace-makers for a problem which is bound to cause the biggest controversy of the 1970 World Cup.

Tours are fun (I hope they stay that way) . . . but the 90 minutes in the concrete canyon of the Aztec Stadium showed they can be valuable, too.

Celtic Chief on Highlights of Club History

Scotland stirred slowly out of its massive annual Hogmanay hang-over on 1 January 1969, to find to its surprise that it had a new football knight.

For overnight Celtic chairman Bob Kelly had become Sir Robert, and even in the often poisonous atmosphere which swirls around as the curse of Scottish football it is fair to say it was an award which brought general approval.

If we are to have an honours system with all its anomalies, there is no doubt that no football legislator deserves it more.

Thousands of people who were not even football fans, never mind Celtic supporters, were happy that a slight to Scotland had at last been rectified.

Despite the awards which had been given to the leading members of the England outfit who won the World Cup there was a genuine anger – and it was amazing that the Government seemed unaware of it for so long – that Celtic as the first British side to win the European Cup had not received one paltry medal in three honours lists after Lisbon.

It was perhaps unfortunate from the public opinion point of view that Sir Matt Busby's knighthood came only a week after his Manchester United had followed Celtic as the second British side to capture the European Cup.

Busby's award, of course, was not just for winning the European Cup, but try telling that to the fan in the pub who could only see it as another example of a deliberate snub to a Scots club.

Equally, Bob Kelly's knighthood was not just because he was chairman of a European Cup winning team. His services to football, even if Celtic had never reached Lisbon, would have merited an honour.

He has been a director of his club since 1931, chairman since 1947, president of the Scottish Football Association and president of the Scottish League, with two terms as president of each body.

You can disagree violently with Bob Kelly, and many have over the years, but on one aspect of his life there is no dispute, his love of football.

He has always put more into the sport than he has ever taken out. One national newspaper columnist greeted his knighthood with the tribute . . . 'his stature exposes the pompous mediocrities who inhabit many boardrooms'.

He could hardly fail to have become interested in football. His father, James Kelly, was Celtic's first captain, after he had been successfully wooed from Renton, the world champions of their era.

'Of course, they thought the world was Britain then,' says Sir Robert.

But, that was after all a long time ago, so how does he manage to maintain his interest in his sixties, at an age when most men confine their activities to feet up in front of a television set. It has meant sitting shivering in an open-air stadium in Belgrade or sweltering in the vast Los Angeles Coliseum.

'I remember asking Alex McNair, who played 21 seasons for us and was a great student of the game, how he kept his interest,' he said.

'He told me "I've never seen a match yet that's not got something new in it." And that's true. I've had a lot of pleasure out of watching Celtic, but any two teams would do, even a match on Glasgow Green.

'When I was a younger man, and the senior season stopped I used to go on to watch junior matches, and then juveniles right through to July. I must have seen hundreds of them, just as long as it was a game of football.'

He can still recall vividly the first time he saw Celtic play . . . the forerunner of literally thousands of times he has seen his team involved.

'It was a Scottish Cup game at Parkhead, around 1911 I think. Bobby Walker scored a great goal for Hearts to give them a 1–0 victory.'

Suddenly the cutlery on the table is re-arranged to describe that goal, and he whisks me back to a time I never knew, of players with

Sir Robert and Lady Kelly . . . with a presentation replica of the most
famous trophy any Scottish club has ever won, the European Cup.

long pants, centre partings, and a whiff of an era packed with the
men who are now football legends.

The move which brought the goal is described in detail, and he
remembers at the end his father, the manager, Willie Maley, and the
famous forward Jimmy McMenemy going out to examine a mud-
mark on one of the posts where some of the Celtic players thought
the ball had crossed the line for the equaliser.

His enthusiasm for one player, of all the hundreds he must have
known, is still undiminished nearly fifty years later.

That player is Patsy Gallacher, the little inside-forward dubbed
by the fans of his day as 'The mighty atom'.

Kelly looks back over a lifetime in football and calls him simply
. . . 'The greatest player I have ever known'.

He gets almost carried away on the memories of Gallacher. I have
heard him defend furiously the legend of the inside-forward in one of

Salute to Sir Robert Kelly . . . from the Celtic stand on New Year's Day. Directors James Farrell and Tom Devlin (front row right) lead the applause for soccer's newest knight.

those late-night discussions when people in football look back and perhaps sigh for their lost youth and old heroes.

Someone had questioned whether or not Gallacher would have succeeded in present-day football, Bob Kelly, for one, had no doubts.

He told me almost wistfully . . . 'I wish he had been captured on film, he had the most perfect balance.'

Suddenly, Sir Robert Kelly, knight of the realm, swoops almost out of his chair in a crowded restaurant to demonstrate to me Gallacher's perfect balance.

He can tell you of moves which led up to Gallacher's goals with such vivid descriptive touches that Jock Stein jokes gently: 'Sometimes I think the chairman adds a defender to these stories.'

Only one modern star has come near to Gallacher in his opinion, and that was Real Madrid's Alfredo Di Stefano, the man Celtic unsuccessfully bid for in the twilight of his great career.

He told me of a discussion he had with Matt Busby, just after Manchester United had brought Denis Law back from Italy to Old Trafford.

'I've just signed the greatest player in the world, in fact the greatest player ever,' said Matt.

He goes on, 'I couldn't accept that.'

'You mean the greatest player you've ever seen,' said Kelly.

'Law is a great player, but not as great as Gallacher. There was one simple test I put to Matt. Gallacher made everyone around him an internationalist, right-half or right-winger . . . you could not say that about Law.'

He talked to me about some of the great Celtic teams, the pre-war Empire Exhibition side of 1938, the Coronation Cup side of 1953 and the European Cup winning side.

Just when it seems he is indulging in the pleasant, but sometimes dangerous pastime of too much nostalgia, he says:

'All great teams. But the European Cup team is the greatest. The other teams reached their peak for around three weeks, the present one has done it over seasons.'

And then he looks to the future, and there is as much excitement in his voice as when he was telling me about the great days so long ago.

'I hope now that we are at the top we can stay on the plateau. We won't win everything, of course, but I think we can recruit the players to keep us there.

'The nucleus of the present team was being built when we were failing to win Cups. It should be easier to stay there now.'

I asked him how he reacted to the period in the sixties when success and Celtic seemed to have fallen out permanently.

When he sat tight-lipped in the front row of the directors' box, and listened to the fans baying for his blood.

'I think a great deal of it was unfair. We were on a youth policy, I personally believe it's the only way for lasting success.

'You can buy players, but to try and buy your way out of permanent trouble just won't work.

'We were beaten in Cup Finals during that time not because I thought we were the worst team but possibly because the players began to think there was a jinx over them.'

Then he traced the thinking which had brought back Jock Stein to Parkhead for the second time, and the real new era of Celtic.

'Jimmy McGrory had been a magnificent servant to Celtic, as a manager and player. But like me he was getting on in years.

'I had always been close to the players. The ones in the teams of the twenties and thirties were my friends.

'I could still talk to the players in the fifties, the ones when Jock played. But by the sixties they looked on me as an old man.

'We needed someone who could talk their language, and we needed to make the change when we had a chance of success.

'It was important the new manager started with a success, and we were going well in the Scottish Cup at the time.'

So Stein returned, to his first triumph with Celtic - the one perhaps forgotten now in the heady victories of Europe but just as important then to the club as any later conquest – the 1965 Scottish Cup win against his old side, Dunfermline.

Bob Kelly's pride when the Celtic come-back was completed as they became the first-ever British team to win the European Cup was evident that night in Lisbon.

Not even an official banquet turned into a babble of Latin voices – and during which he had threatened to sit down if they didn't shut up during his speech – had dimmed his pleasure.

That was evident when he arrived back at the team's luxury hotel headquarters, the Palace Hotel in Estoril – holiday home of millionaires – after the game and that long drawn-out banquet.

It's doubtful if the lofty hotel had ever seen a night like it. Yet such is the irony of success in football that possibly many of the fans offering him their congratulations would have been happy only a few short years before that to see him quit.

However, maybe because the greater part of his life has been spent at a time when, both in a football and political sense, Britain did not need Europe, he has never fallen completely under the spell of the Continental trophies.

That's in contrast to his manager, Jock Stein, who thrives in Europe and sees it as the great challenge of modern football.

That fertile mind of the Celtic manager ticks over to find new ways of getting the maximum advantage out of the speed of jet travel . . . that's why his team are now whisked home the night of a game in Europe if the kick-off is suitably early.

Just about Stein's unhappiest spell in football was in the autumn of 1967 when Celtic lost first to Dynamo Kiev in the European Cup, and then the disaster of the World championship against Racing.

It meant that Celtic were forced to take a back seat and clear off the soccer stage that Stein loves most of all for his team . . . Europe!

However his chairman is more cautious. As far back as 1964 he was writing in a newspaper that he would like to see a British Cup – not a British league – but a knock-out competition with the top eight clubs from Scotland and England.

'I think we have more to offer Europe than they have to offer us, so we should be very careful,' Sir Robert told me.

Perhaps one day the domestic fixture lists will be trimmed to allow a British Cup. Certainly clashes between teams from the two

Salute to Sir Robert Kelly . . . a toast from the Rangers' directors after
the match against Celtic at Ibrox on 2 January. The boardroom line-up
(*left to right*) . . . Rangers' directors, George Brown, David Hope, Chairman
John Lawrence, Sir Robert Kelly, Matt Taylor and Ian McLaren.

countries, in any of the Continental trophies, has aroused frantic
interest.

Yet it's precisely because his commitment to Europe is not so
complete that his criticisms of the tournaments run just now have
validity.

'I don't like two-legged ties, and I never have done. I think they
are against the right spirit of football, which is to win over 90
minutes.

'My father used to say: "It doesn't take a good team to stop a
good team." And that's what you get with emphasis on defence in
these games.

'And I don't like either teams tossing a coin to decide who wins
a game, or winning matches because away goals count double. These
are not in the laws of football, they are only designed to avoid fixture
problems.'

No one can deny that, at some time, the European authorities will
have to examine all these points, no matter how much they are
swept under the soccer carpet just now.

And if some of his campaigns, like the team selections when he was virtual boss at Parkhead, have seemed a little eccentric he has the comforting knowledge that other campaigns, for which he was wildly unpopular at the time, have been proved right.

Sir Robert has a rich West of Scotland accent, and a habit of raising his voice to harangue his listeners.

But it was never raised louder than in his long-running battle against the live televising of matches, as a menace to the future of football.

He had seen the damage, on trips to America, that TV had done to attendances at actual sports events, such as boxing and baseball.

And he was determined to fight it over here, although it meant putting himself in a position where at the time he had few friends.

Now, although TV and soccer have learned to live, sometimes uneasily, with each other many would agree that he was proved right to point out the dangers 'the box' can have for sport.

Nearly nine years ago he wanted a total ban for one year on anyone connected with football even appearing on TV, and he still holds to that extreme view today.

His argument is simply expressed: 'I think television needs football more than we need TV. A black-out for one year would prove who was right.'

He told me of negotiations over ten years ago with the TV authorities when they wanted regularly to show live league games, an event which has not yet happened.

'They offered a trifling sum. I told them to come back and talk when they were ready to offer a sum, say sixpence a head, for every viewer who watched the match.'

The man on the terracing has a champion in the Celtic chairman.

'Football needs people in the grounds to make it successful, to give it atmosphere. I don't see why the fans who go to a ground, pay for their travelling and admission, and in cases of big games probably have a lot of trouble to obtain a ticket, should subsidise TV viewers who are only prepared to watch football from their own home.'

The decision of the four home associations to allow their kick-off times of the British international championship to be manipulated for TV coverage was quickly dismissed.

'I can't understand it. It's an incredible decision. I certainly would never have allowed it in my time as president of the S.F.A. or League.'

Yet Bob Kelly's views, which must appear ultra-conservative to the TV authorities, can be surprisingly forward looking on other aspects.

Salute to Sir Robert Kelly . . . a standing ovation from the S.F.A.
Council, including ex-president Tom Reid.

He is devoutly religious yet I have heard him tell a press conference
in America that eventually he considers some form of Sunday sport
will come to Britain.

And it is typical of the man that when I asked him what he would
most like to see done to improve football there were no vague
theories . . . the answer was swift and direct.

'An improvement in referees to stamp out rough play and the
courage of the top authorities to back them up,' he said.

'My great fear is the growing number of young players who come up
on disciplinary charges, I know that from the Referees Committee.

'But you can't blame them. They go to watch international matches,
and they see dreadful fouls committed by star players.

'In the old days if a player misbehaved in an international there
was only one course, he just wasn't picked again.

'I think that's what's got to happen now. The authorities have
closed their eyes for too long to what's happening.

'Football is not a namby-pamby game. No one wants to see all the fire taken out of it. But I think there's a limit, and it's been reached.

'This is not something which has just happened in a season. I remember the "Battle of Berne" in the 1954 World Cup between Hungary and Brazil.

'There was only one answer to that, both teams should have been expelled from the tournament.'

It explains why after that World championship punch-up in Montevideo between Celtic and Racing Club, the Parkhead players were each fined £200.

And it was no window-dressing or exercise in public relations. The money was whipped off their wages. . . .

That was perhaps his worst moment as chairman. But there have been many, many more marvellous moments to make up for it since that winter's day in 1911 when he first saw his team play.

Some of us used to believe that his sometimes brusque and even autocratic manner with questioners made him almost unapproachable.

But in recent years, perhaps because he had freed himself of the responsibility of running the team – and it's something many directors could copy – he has mellowed into an elder statesman of football.

Not one without a bite, no one could ever imagine that, and doubtless there will be times when he is wrong in his views.

But anybody who has ever attended an S.F.A. council meeting, 'the parliament of football', and watched the quality of legislators knows how high Kelly stands above most of them,

The development of modern soccer was something that not even the most visionary of Celtic's founders could have imagined when they signed up James Kelly in 1888, but his son has adjusted to most of the changes.

Sir Robert Kelly summed up simply the centre of his thinking in an era when too many people look on football as a mere business sideline with attractive perks in the shape of big match tickets and foreign trips, by telling me. . . .

'A director must be a fan as well.'

And he has certainly been that!